CLUB MIILFF

Leah Forster
Club Miilff

Published by Spines
ISBN: 979-8-89569-454-1

CLUB MIILFF

LEAH FORSTER

DEDICATION

She calls me love.

Dearest Reader

Club Miilff is a fiction. If there are characters that seem familiar to you, good! That means there were pieces of this book that were relatable, and that was my intent. Here's to every MIILFF I know and the many I can't wait to meet –I wrote every word with you in mind.

Leah

CONTENTS

CHAPTER ONE
THE MIILFF REVOLUTION

The studio of "Call Her Mommy" thrummed with electric anticipation. Host Alexis Hooper's voice, a blend of honey and mischief, purred through millions of headphones worldwide.

"Mommy Gang, buckle up those Spanx, because today's guest is about to flip your world faster than you can say 'baby bottle.' She's a successful female who turned 'MILF' from a sleazy acronym into a battle cry for empowerment. She's not just a board member of CLUB MIILFF, *Mothers interested in Launching Financial Freedom*, she is also the CEO who built a $2.3 billion empire by teaching women to dominate boardrooms and bedrooms with equal ferocity. Ladies, gentlemen, and everyone in between – meet the woman who puts the 'bad' in badass mom, Leah Hart!"

Leah leaned into the mic, her gravelly voice sending shivers through the airwaves. "What's up, Mommy Gang?"

Hooper's eyes widened, drinking in Leah's presence. The MIILFF queen exuded an intoxicating blend of sharp angles and soft curves, her crisp white shirt unbuttoned just enough to reveal a tantalizing glimpse of tattoos. She radiated a raw, androgynous magnetism that defied labels and left everyone wanting more.

"Damn, Leah, you are everyone's type, aren't you?" Alexis purred. "Speaking of types, I'm loving that pizza slice tattoo. What's the story there?"

For a moment, Leah's eyes clouded over...

"You're getting fat, Layla," her mother's voice echoed in her ears.

A shadow flickered across Leah's face...

"Layla, you are disgusting fat slob," Her mother's voice cut like a knife. "No dinner for you. Maybe then you'll lose that baby fat."

Teenage Leah's fingers trembled as she counted out five hard-earned quarters. The pizza slice she'd buy would be more than food — it was her first taste of rebellion.

Leah's ocean eyes refocused, a dangerous glint replacing the momentary vulnerability. "Let's just say, Alexis, that this little slice represents the moment I realized I'm definitely pie sexual. I love that dough!"

Leah had the tenacity of Mel and Tony Robbins, the wit of a younger Jerry Seinfeld and the leadership skills of Simon Sinek. Plus, she was hot, genuine, talented, and people were always fascinated by her unique Ultra-Orthodox Hasidic upbringing. What always seemed to shock them was that despite her trauma, she chose devout observance as a practicing Jew. What shocked people even more? She was also an out lesbian and very much in love with a popular New York City female cardiologist.

Leah teetered a lot. She dangled between being a Millennial/ Gen Xer and being a part of a progressive community, and having loads of conservative friends and chosen family. She was too "frum" for some and not religious enough for others. Yet Leah walked the line thoughtfully.

Alexis leaned in, completely enthralled. "Okay, you magnificent MIILFF, I'm hooked. Spill it. How does a girl go from sneaking pizza into her room to running a billion-dollar empire and reclaiming such an awful disgrace of a word?"

Leah's lips curled into a wolfish grin. "Picture this: Brooklyn, five years ago. I'm suffocating in another power suit, wondering if my son is doing ok in college." She laughed uncomfortably. "Yep, I have a college kid. And I know I look young, but in corporate years, I'm a senior."

The way she said senior excited Alexis.

The studio faded away as Leah's story unfurled. Across the globe, millions of listeners leaned in, pulses quickening. This wasn't just an interview – it was the opening salvo of a revolution. There were future MIILFFs everywhere in the world, and Leah was speaking directly to each one of them.

"It's funny," she started.

"It all kinda began with …Poga!"

Chapter Two
Poga and Paradigm Shifts

Breathe
Breathe it in, Breathe it out.
Let it go.
Let. It. GO.
Leah laughed to herself, and she dug her feet further into the sand.
Yoga.
Now that's legit.
But…Poga? That's a different story entirely!

The scent of lavender oil and questionable life choices hung heavy in the air as Leah cautiously entered the studio. The soft glow of Himalayan salt lamps cast an otherworldly pink hue across the room, transforming the space into something between a yoga studio and a trendy nightclub.

Mats of various colors were arranged in a circular pattern, each one facing a gleaming silver pole that stretched from floor to ceiling.

Leah's heart pounded in her chest, a mixture of excitement and trepidation coursing through her veins. She took a deep breath, trying to center herself.

Why am I doing this? I'm 42. I have no business attending a class called POGA.

POGA. Just when you thought fitness crazes had reached maximum level nutty, some mid-twenties "health coach" influencer in New York City tagged POGA in a post and ranted about how this life-changing class transformed her mental and physical health. The post had gone viral faster than a cat video, and suddenly, every wellness junkie from Brooklyn to the Bronx was clamoring for a spot in these elusive classes.

And here was Leah, swept up in the madness, sporting a fresh pair of Lululemon leggings that still had the price tag tucked discreetly in the waistband. She placed her sneakers to the side in a woven bamboo bin, her fingers lingering on the soft leather as if reluctant to let go of this last connection to the normal world outside.

Glancing at her reflection in the floor-to-ceiling POGA studio mirror, Leah barely recognized herself. Gone was the timid, rule-following woman of her past. In her place stood someone daring, someone willing to try something as outlandish as POGA. But the dark circles under her eyes spoke volumes, a testament to nights spent tossing and turning, worrying about her child miles away at college.

As she stared at her reflection, her inner critic began to shout, its voice a cacophony of doubt and self-recrimination.

You should be sleeping better -- but instead, you're tossing and turning at night worrying about your 20-year-old! Your kid is finally in college, Leah. You did it! And guess what? This is YOUR time! You're 42! You raised your kid when you were young. Was it hard? YES! But look at you! You have a great career, you're healthy, you're in therapy, AND you still have your whole life ahead of you! You're lucky, Leah! Start focusing on yourself and stop hyper-fixating on your son. Jack is fine. Are you fine?

Leah shook her head, trying to silence the relentless stream of thoughts. She was here now, wasn't she? Taking a step towards something new, something for herself. That had to count for something.

"Hello, beautiful POGA people!"

A loud yet lilting voice interrupted Leah's harsh self-critique, startling her out of her reverie. She turned to see a willowy figure gliding into the center of the room, bare feet barely making a sound on the polished hardwood floor.

The woman was a vision in flowing white linen, her crop top revealing a toned midriff adorned with a delicate belly chain. Her hair was a riot of dreadlocks, decorated with tiny seashells and wooden beads that clinked softly as she moved. But it was her eyes that captured Leah's attention - kohl-rimmed and intense, they seemed to look right through her as if peering into her very soul.

"Gorgeous humans, my name is Reighbeuo." She paused for effect, her gaze sweeping across the room with an intensity that made Leah want to squirm. "That's spelled R-E-I-G-H, as in our highest self has the power to REIGN over our suffering egos!"

Leah blinked, processing the information. Reighbeuo, not Rainbow. She got it. She glanced around, relieved to see equally bewildered expressions on the faces of her fellow classmates.

The instructor dramatically paced around the room, her movements fluid and graceful. She paused to wave a bundle of smoking sage, its pungent aroma mixing with the lavender to create a scent that was part New Age bookshop, part grandmother's linen closet.

"Pole," Reighbeuo intoned, her voice dropping to a near whisper, "is about balance." She paused again, the silence in the room so complete you could hear a pin drop. "Yoga!" Her voice rose to a crescendo, making Leah jump slightly. "Yoga is about balance. Today, we shall balance our mind and body as we fuse sensuality with mindfulness."

Leah fumbled with her mat, a garishly pink affair she'd impulse-bought online, wondering what possessed her to enter a room where words like "sensuality" and "mindfulness" were being thrown about in casual terms. She felt out of her depth, like a fish suddenly asked to climb a tree.

As she struggled to unroll her mat without drawing attention to herself, a figure materialized beside her. Leah looked up, her eyes traveling from a pair of perfectly pedicured toes, up long, toned legs, to meet a pair of bright blue eyes that could charm a cobra.

The woman smiled infectiously, her short, spiky hair giving her an elfin quality that was both striking and approachable. "Mel," she offered, extending a hand adorned with an intricate henna design. "First timer too?"

Leah sheepishly nodded, accepting the handshake. "Is it that obvious?"

Mel chuckled, a warm, rich sound that immediately put Leah at ease. "The muttering under your breath gave it away. Plus, you look about as comfortable as a straight girl in Henrietta Hudson."

The gayest bar in New York City.

Leah felt a flush creep up her neck. "That obvious, huh? I feel like I've stumbled into some sort of mystical circus. Half expecting someone to start juggling crystals any minute now."

Mel's eyes twinkled with mirth. "Oh, don't give them ideas. I wouldn't put it past our illustrious leader over there," she said, nodding towards Reighbeuo, who was now demonstrating what appeared to be a fusion of a sun salutation and a pole dance move.

Just as Leah was about to respond, a whirlwind of energy inserted itself on the mat next to her. A striking woman, donning leopard-print leggings that left little to the imagination, settled into a perfect split. Her long, messy hair was the color of spun caramel, and her red lipstick, though slightly smudged, somehow made her look more alluring rather than disheveled.

She eyed Mel with intent, quickly performing a once-over as Mel awkwardly adjusted her posture. "You two better stop yapping," she chided with a playful tone, her thick Brooklyn accent adding to her spicy energy. "Rainbow Bright over here takes her POGA very seriously."

The three of them suppressed snorts of laughter as Reighbeuo continued her introduction, her voice carried on a cloud of patchouli. "We will begin with a POGA POSE -- think Child's pose, but against the pole. Touch your pole, say hello to your pole -- connect with your pole."

The newcomer rolled her eyes, her voice a conspiratorial whisper. "She's got us talking to our poles. What's next? Asking it out for dinner and a movie?"

"And I paid 43 dollars for this class!" Leah chimed in, her voice a mix of disbelief and amusement. "You gotta love Brooklyn. Where else can you pay top dollar to fondle fitness equipment?"

Mel suppressed her laugh, her shoulders shaking with the effort. "Okay, at least I'm not the only crazy one! Does she actually think I'm going to talk to a pole? I mean, I signed up because I wanna try new things, but…"

Leah finished Mel's sentence with a dramatic imitation of Reighbeuo's voice, "But POGA is about balance!" She waggled her eyebrows for emphasis, causing both Mel and the newcomer to dissolve into giggles.

As they attempted to follow Reighbeuo's increasingly outlandish instructions, Leah found herself warming to her new acquaintances.

There was something liberating about sharing this absurd experience with others, about being able to laugh at themselves and the situation they'd found themselves in.

During a particularly challenging pose that had Leah convinced her spine was trying to exit her body through her left ear, she found herself opening up. "You know," she grunted, attempting to maintain her balance, "I never thought I'd be here. A year ago, I was still trying to figure out how to be a single mom to a teenager. Now my kid is in college, and I'm... well, I'm talking to a pole."

Mel, who was faring slightly better but still looked like a pretzel with limbs, nodded sympathetically. "Life has a way of throwing curveballs, doesn't it? One minute, you're sure you've got it all figured out, the next, you're in a POGA class wondering if you've completely lost the plot."

The woman in the leopard-print leggings, who had introduced herself as Natasha, chimed in. "Honey, if you think you've got it all figured out, you're probably doing it wrong. Lives are meant to be a hot mess. Embrace the chaos!"

As they moved through the poses, their conversation deepened, revealing layers of complexity in each of their lives. Their introductions became a tapestry of unspoken stories, each woman sharing snippets of her past and present.

Leah, between deep breaths and wobbling attempts at balance, shared more of her story. "I was raised in a Hasidic community," she said, her voice low as if sharing a secret. "Arranged marriage at 18, mother by 19. It was... suffocating. When I finally left, it was like learning to breathe all over again."

She paused, gathering her thoughts before continuing. "I raised my child alone after my family and community wanted nothing to do with a formerly orthodox wife who had the audacity to leave her husband for a woman after a horrible 12-year marriage. I spent my entire 20s and 30s being a mom and handling an alcoholic husband, and then rebounded badly with the first girl I fell for. I totally collapsed into a codependent and super toxic relationship with her, and now, I'm actually dating someone I like... I think? " She laughed, a bit embarrassed. "But what do I know about healthy relationships? I'm learning as I go!"

Mel's eyes widened with interest and empathy. "That must have been incredibly difficult. How did you manage?"

Leah chuckled, a sound tinged with both mirth and a hint of old pain. "One day at a time. And a lot of therapy. And Yoga. Oh, and questionable fashion choices. You should have seen my first attempt at 'modern' clothing. I looked like I'd raided the clearance rack at five different stores." She smiled. "Did I say yoga?"

Natasha, executing a perfect split while the other two struggled to touch their toes, nodded approvingly. "Fashion faux pas are a rite of passage, darling. I once wore a neon green tube top with plaid pants to a job interview. I didn't get the job, but I did get a date with the receptionist."

This elicited a burst of laughter from Leah and Mel, drawing a sharp look from Reighbeuo, who was in the middle of demonstrating a pose she called "The Awakened."

As they moved into a less demanding stretch, Mel took the opportunity to share her own story. "I'm a writer," she said, her voice tinged with a mix of pride and frustration. "Or at least, I was. This damn writers' strike has left me with more free time than I know what to do with and a bank account that's screaming for mercy."

Leah nodded sympathetically. "That must be tough. What do you write?"

Mel's face lit up, her passion evident. "TV scripts, mostly. I was working on a new series about a misunderstood group of people and their ties to the Jewelry district."

Natasha raised an eyebrow, her lips curving into an amused smile. "Jewelry? Now that's a show I'd binge-watch. Throw in a steamy love triangle and a tall man in finance, and I'm sold."

Leah immediately began chanting the viral TikTok sound. "I'm looking for a man in finance."

Natasha laughed and continued, "6.5. Blue Eyes."

Mel caved. "Trust fund!"

They burst out laughing.

As Mel laughed, her cheeks flushing slightly. "Or a woman. I'm open to either." She laughed. "Or both."

She paused, her expression growing more serious. "But it's not just the strike. I've spent my entire life experiencing polyamorous relationships. I travel a lot and meet people everywhere I go. I've dated men, women, and everything in between, and yet, this past year, I can honestly say I just feel lonely. I find myself constantly asking, 'What's next... what now?'"

Leah reached out, giving Mel's arm a supportive squeeze. "I get that. It's like we're all trying to find our place, you know? Figure out who we are beyond the roles we've played."

Natasha nodded, her usual bravado softening for a moment. "Ain't that the truth? We're all just making it up as we go along, pretending we've got it all figured out."

As the class progressed, Natasha remained an enigma shrouded in more enigma. She would offer vague responses about what she did for work, hinting at having a fantastic life that was anything but ordinary. "I guess you can call me an independent consultant of some sort," she said with a wink, leaving Leah and Mel to wonder what exactly that entailed.

Despite the absurdity of POGA (and Reighbeuo's questionable taste in music), a connection sparked between the three women. As they grappled with gravity, balance, and their own insecurities, laughter filled the air, forging an instant bond that came more naturally to Leah than the downward-facing panther that Reighbeuo was demonstrating.

"Apparently, panthers are way more sensual than dogs. Who knew?" Mel whispered, causing Leah to snort with laughter and nearly topple over.

By the end of the class, muscles screaming and spirits surprisingly high, Leah knew she had shown up that day to experience something more than a POGA class. The last hour in the studio was about stepping outside her comfort zone, embracing the ridiculous, and finding new connections in the most unexpected places.

As soon as POGA was over, Natasha, followed by her tropical aroma storm of mango and mischief, sashayed over to Leah and Mel. As they wiped down their sweaty mats, Mel and Leah exchanged glances, silently acknowledging the spectrum of life experiences Natasha's mere presence implied.

Leah, the ex-religious wife and mother, is still navigating the uncharted territory of freedom. Mel, the writer, is grappling with a stagnant career, restlessness, and possibly, as hinted by the silver ring on her finger, a non-monogamous relationship. Natasha was a quirky ball of oddness, radiating an energy that promised both intrigue and potential chaos.

"So, ladies," Natasha purred, her voice low and enticing, "up for an adventure tomorrow night?"

Mel's eyebrows shot up, suspicion battling curiosity in her eyes. Leah, however, felt a spark of adrenaline ignite in her chest. Feeling a newfound boldness she didn't recognize, she blurted, "Depends on the adventure!"

Natasha winked, her crooked lipstick-smudged smile hinting at secrets untold. "Trust me, toots," she said, the old-fashioned endearment rolling off her tongue. "You want to be there."

She reached into her bag, movements deliberate and theatrical and pulled out a small white envelope. "The details are in here."

Mel, ever the skeptic, reached for the envelope and slowly removed a simple white card. Her eyes widened as she read the words printed in elegant script: "Club MIILFF." Her reaction was immediate -- obvious disdain mixed with a reluctant curiosity. "MILF? Really?"

Natasha chuckled, her laugh a rich, throaty sound that drew glances from across the room. "Oh, come on, Miss Bisexual Polyamorous POGA student, don't act like you're so rigid. This club is magic. All I'm going to say is, be ready for something unforgettable." Her gum cracked, punctuating her words like an exclamation point.

Still skeptical, Mel turned the card over, her journalist's instincts kicking in. On the back was a QR code, sleek and mysterious.

Natasha gave them both a quick once-over, her eyes gleaming with mischief. "Scan that barcode. You'll find all the details you need." She leaned in close, her voice dropping to a conspiratorial whisper. "But fair warning, ladies – once you step through those doors, there's no going back."

Before they could pepper her with follow-up questions, Natasha sashayed away, unabashedly readjusting her leggings as she muttered, "Wedgie check!" She left behind the mysterious invitation and a cryptic last glance that seemed to say, "The choice is yours."

Mel and Leah exchanged confused glances, the white card between them suddenly feeling like a ticking time bomb of potential.

"MIILFF?" Mel queried again, a mix of amusement and apprehension in her voice. "What do you think the extra 'I' and 'F' stand for?"

Leah shrugged, a grin slowly spreading across her face. The adrenaline from the POGA class was still coursing through her veins, making her feel bold and adventurous. "Well, Mel," she said, surprising herself with her eagerness, "looks like we're not just defying expectations anymore. We're embracing them." She winked a sparkle in her eye that hadn't been there when she first walked into the studio.

Mel couldn't help but laugh, shaking her head in disbelief. "I can't believe I'm even considering this. A few hours ago, I was sitting in my apartment, wallowing in writer's block and self-pity. Now I'm contemplating going to some mysterious club with two women I just met in a POGA class. Has the world gone mad, or is it just me?"

Leah grinned, feeling a connection with Mel that went beyond their shared POGA experience. "Maybe a little bit of both? But you know what? It feels good to be a little mad sometimes. To do something unexpected."

As they gathered their things, the energy in the studio began to shift. Other POGA participants were filing out, their faces a mix of exhaustion and exhilaration. Reighbeuo was in the corner, carefully extinguishing her incense and humming what sounded suspiciously like a Britney Spears song.

Leah and Mel found themselves lingering, neither quite ready to burst the bubble of possibility that had formed around them. They moved to the small lounge area near the entrance, collapsing onto a plush velvet couch that seemed at odds with the studio's otherwise minimalist decor.

"So," Leah said, turning to face Mel, "tell me more about the concept you're working on!"

Mel's face lit up, her earlier melancholy forgotten in the face of discussing her passion project. "Oh, where do I even start? It's a mix of historical drama and a coming-of-age story. The main character, she's... complicated."

As Mel launched into a detailed description of her characters and plot twists, Leah found herself captivated. She could almost see the scenes playing out in her mind – Sylvia and her team of misfit librarians jumping through time, armed with nothing but their knowledge of literature and a well-stocked bookmobile.

"That sounds amazing," Leah said when Mel finally paused for breath. "I'd watch the hell out of that show. How is it not already on Netflix?"

Mel's excitement dimmed slightly. "That's the dream. But you know how it is in this industry. It's all about who you know and having the right connections. And with the strike..." She trailed off, shrugging helplessly.

Leah nodded, understanding all too well the frustration of feeling stuck, of having dreams just out of reach. "Hey, you never know. Maybe this MIILFF thing will be full of TV executives looking for the next big hit."

They both laughed at the absurdity of the idea, but there was a note of hope in their laughter. After all, stranger things had happened. Hadn't they just spent an hour doing yoga poses named after exotic animals while clutching metal poles?

As their laughter subsided, a comfortable silence fell between them. Leah found herself studying Mel's profile, noticing the way her short hair curled slightly at the nape of her neck, the determined set of her jaw. There was something about her that drew Leah in, a kindred spirit in this crazy, mixed-up world.

"What about you?" Mel asked suddenly, turning to meet Leah's gaze. "What's your story? I mean, beyond the whole ex-Hasidic, single mom thing. What makes Leah tick?"

Leah felt a flutter in her stomach, unused to being the center of such focused attention. "Oh, you know," she said, aiming for nonchalance, "just your average 42-year-old trying to figure out who she is now that her kid's flown the nest. No big deal."

Mel raised an eyebrow, clearly not buying the casual act. "Come on, there's got to be more to it than that. What do you do when you're not attending questionable fitness classes or worrying about your child?"

Leah laughed, caught out. "Is it that obvious that I'm a professional worrier?" She paused, considering the question seriously. "I work in IT, actually. Cybersecurity. It's about as far from my old life as you can get, which I guess was the point when I chose it."

"Wow," Mel said, genuinely impressed. "That's badass. So, you're like, what, a hacker?"

"More like an anti-hacker," Leah corrected with a smile. "I help companies protect themselves from cyber-attacks. It's challenging work, always changing. Keeps me on my toes."

"I bet," Mel nodded. "But is that what you always wanted to do? When you were a little girl in your Hasidic community, did you dream of firewalls and encryption?"

Leah laughed, the sound tinged with a hint of melancholy. "Not exactly. I wanted to be a writer. I used to scribble stories in the margins of my prayer books, much to my teacher's dismay."

"No kidding?" Mel's eyes lit up. "What kind of stories?"

"Fantasy, mostly," Leah admitted, feeling a blush creep up her neck. "Stories about girls who could fly, who could change the world with a word. Girls who were free." She paused to reflect and smiled sheepishly, "Girls who kissed girls." She blushed deeper.

The weight of that admission hung in the air between them. Mel reached out, squeezing Leah's hand gently. "Sounds like you were writing your own future."

Leah squeezed back, feeling a connection spark between them. "Maybe I was. Didn't know it at the time, though."

As they sat there, hands linked, the world around them seemed to fade away. The bustling sounds of the studio, the lingering scent of incense, all became background noise to the electricity humming between them.

The ping broke the moment of a notification from Mel's phone. She reluctantly let go of Leah's hand to check it, her brow furrowing as she read the message.

"Everything okay?" Leah asked, immediately concerned.

Mel sighed, running a hand through her spiky hair. "Yeah, just... writer stuff. My agent reminded me that even though we're on strike, I should be using this time to 'stay creative' and 'build my brand'." She made air quotes around the phrases, her voice dripping with sarcasm.

"Sounds stressful," Leah sympathized. "Is that why you decided to try POGA? To stay creative?"

Mel laughed, the tension leaving her shoulders. "God, no. I came because my therapist suggested I try something new, something physical to get me out of my head. I think her exact words were, Mel, if you don't leave your apartment soon, you're going to merge with your couch and become some kind of writer-furniture hybrid.'"

They both dissolved into giggles at the image, the stress of the outside world momentarily forgotten.

As their laughter subsided, Leah found herself glancing at the white card still clutched in Mel's hand. The mystery of Club MIILFF beckoned, a siren calls of adventure and possibility.

"So," she said, nodding towards the card, "what do you think? Should we do it? Take a chance on whatever madness Natasha's inviting us to?"

Mel bit her lip, clearly torn. "I don't know. It could be anything. A pyramid scheme, a cult, a weird book club..."

"Or," Leah countered, feeling bolder by the second, "it could be the start of something amazing. A chance to step outside our comfort zones, to be the protagonists in our own stories for once."

Mel studied Leah's face, seeming to search for something. Whatever she saw there must have convinced her because she nodded slowly. "You know what? You're right. Let's do it. Let's embrace the madness."

With that decision made, a surge of excitement coursed through both. They quickly exchanged numbers, making plans to meet the next evening before heading to the mysterious club.

As they finally left the studio, stepping out into the bustling New York evening, Leah felt as though she was seeing the world through new eyes. The city thrummed with energy and possibility, mirroring the excitement bubbling in her chest.

Mel and Leah parted ways at the subway station, each heading home to prepare for whatever adventure awaited them the next night. As Leah watched Mel disappear into the crowd, she felt a sense of anticipation she hadn't experienced in years.

That night, as Leah lay in bed, her muscles aching pleasantly from the POGA class, she found her thoughts drifting not to her child or her worries, but to the possibilities that tomorrow might bring. For the first time in a long time, she fell asleep with a smile on her face, dreaming of complicated characters and exclusive clubs where anything was possible.

Little did she know that the adventure awaiting her at Club MIILFF would be beyond anything she could have imagined. The POGA class was just the beginning. The real journey – one that would challenge her, thrill her, and ultimately transform her – was about to begin.

As the city that never sleeps pulsed around her, Leah slept soundly, blissfully unaware that her life was about to change forever.

Tomorrow, she would step into a world of intrigue, empowerment, and unexpected alliances. Tomorrow, she would begin to discover who Leah truly was, beyond the roles of mother, ex-Hasidic woman, and IT professional.

Tomorrow, the real adventure would begin.

Chapter Three
The MIILFF's Lair

The Brooklyn night hummed with secrets, its shadows cloaking the nondescript building Leah and Mel approached. The streetlights cast an eerie glow on the wet pavement, remnants of an earlier drizzle that had left the air thick with the scent of rain and urban mystery. A distant siren wailed, a reminder of the city that never sleeps, always pulsing with life and intrigue.

Leah, a caffeine queen clutching her venti Starbucks like a lifeline, winked conspiratorially at Mel. "Addiction? Moi?" she quipped, her voice a mixture of self-deprecation and unapologetic indulgence. The steam from her cup curled upwards, mingling with the misty air, creating an ephemeral halo around her head.

Mel, perpetually cool in her charcoal beanie and wreathed in a thin veil of cigarette smoke, muttered about wishing she could quit nicotine. "It's a love-hate relationship," she sighed, flicking ash onto the sidewalk. "Mostly hate these days, but old habits die hard, you know?"

Leah nodded sympathetically, her eyes drawn to the graceful way Mel held her cigarette, fingers long and artistic. There was something undeniably alluring about Mel's brooding writer vibe, even if the habit itself was less than ideal.

Fashion, as always, spoke volumes about their personalities. Leah, ever the fashionista, sported a stylish tan trench coat that hugged her curves in all the right places. It was cinched at the waist with a wide belt, giving her an hourglass silhouette that turned heads as they walked. Her hair, a cascade of carefully tousled waves, framed her face perfectly, catching the golden glow of the streetlights.

Mel, in stark contrast, radiated effortless androgyny in a simple black short jacket. The leather was soft and worn, speaking of years of use and cherished memories. Her outfit was completed with slim-fit dark jeans and scuffed combat boots that had clearly seen their fair share of adventures. The overall effect was one of casual coolness, as if she had thrown on the first things she found in her closet and somehow managed to look like she'd stepped out of an indie rock band's album cover, with no bra.

As they neared the building, its facade blending seamlessly with the surrounding architecture, Mel's pace slowed. Her brow furrowed, etching lines of concern across her forehead. "Almost chickened out," she confessed, her voice barely audible over the city's constant thrum of traffic and distant conversations.

Leah turned to her new friend, concern evident in her eyes. "What's wrong? Having second thoughts about our little adventure?"

Mel shrugged, a gesture that spoke volumes about her inner turmoil. "It's just... Google painted a pretty murky picture of this whole 'MILF' thing, you know? And me, I'm not a mother by any stretch of the imagination. Hell, I can barely keep a plant alive." She let out a self-deprecating chuckle. "I just keep thinking, what am I doing here? This is exactly how I felt 30 seconds before walking into that POGA class. Like, why am I here again? I'm not even a mom!"

Leah reached out, giving Mel's arm a reassuring squeeze. "Hey, we're in this together, remember? Whatever this turns out to be, we'll face it as a team. Besides, after surviving Reighbeuo and her 'Sensual Sloth' pose, I think we can handle just about anything."

Mel's lips quirked into a small smile, some of the tension easing from her shoulders. "You're right. I mean, what could be worse than trying to look graceful while essentially hugging a metal pole?"

Their moment of camaraderie was suddenly interrupted by a voice that sliced through the air like a perfectly sharpened knife. "Nervous, newbies?"

Both women turned to see Natasha materialize from the shadows, a vision in red spandex that clung to her curves like a second skin. Her lips, painted a shade of crimson that matched her outfit perfectly, curved into a knowing smirk. She exuded confidence and sex appeal in equal measure, drawing the eye like a magnet.

Natasha's gaze settled on Mel, her expression a mixture of amusement and something deeper, more predatory. "Trust me, there's a difference between lying and omitting the truth. Ask anyone in politics." She paused dramatically, her eyes taking on a faraway look. "Actually, ask anyone. Including my ex-husband. Who, till this very day, mind you, claims he never 'actually' cheated because I never asked him if we were exclusive."

Leah and Mel exchanged glances, caught off guard by this sudden outpouring of personal information. Natasha, however, was on a roll.

"I mean, pardon me for thinking we were exclusive when he asked, practically begged me to MARRY him!" She threw her hands up in exasperation, her bracelets jangling musically with the movement. "Men, I swear. They think with their little heads and then act surprised when we call them out on their bullshit."

Mel, looking increasingly uncomfortable, shifted her weight from one foot to the other. Natasha, picking up on her discomfort, softened her approach slightly. "Look, Mel, think of this like telling your boss you're 'running late' when you're hungover. Omission, toots." She winked, her words laced with sly amusement.

Again, with the 'toots,' Mel thought, resisting the urge to roll her eyes. There was something about Natasha that both intrigued and irritated her, a combination that left her feeling off-balance and slightly on edge.

Leah, on the other hand, was practically vibrating with excitement. She'd never been to anything this mysterious and cool before. The secretive nature of the club, the enigmatic invitation, and even Natasha's over-the-top persona all added up to an adventure unlike anything she'd experienced in her previous life.

As they approached the entrance, Leah's mind wandered back to her days in the Hasidic community. How different this was from the structured, predictable life she'd left behind. Every day, there was a set pattern, and ancient laws and traditions guided every decision. Here, in the heart of Brooklyn, she was stepping into the unknown, embracing the thrill of uncertainty. The contrast was both exhilarating and terrifying.

They entered the building, the air thick with anticipation and the faint scent of perfume and possibility. The lobby was surprisingly nondescript – beige walls, generic potted plants, and a security desk that looked like it had seen better days. A stern-faced bodyguard, her muscular arms folded across her chest, stood behind the desk. Her eyes, sharp and assessing, scanned each of them in turn.

"Invitations," she grunted, her voice gravelly and no-nonsense.

Natasha stepped forward, producing the white envelopes with a flourish. "Right here, sugar. Three new initiates for Club MIILFF."

The guard's eyebrow raised a fraction of an inch at Natasha's familiarity, but she said nothing. Instead, she pulled out a sleek, high-tech scanner and ran it over the barcodes on each invitation. There was a moment of tense silence as the device processed the information, broken only by the soft beep of confirmation.

As the guard handed back the invitations, her gaze lingered on Mel. There was a subtle shift in her expression, a softening around the eyes that spoke of interest and appreciation. Mel, lost in her own thoughts and nerves, never noticed the attention. Somehow, her obliviousness to her own appeal made her even more attractive, a fact not lost on either Leah or Natasha.

Just as they were about to move past the security desk, the relative calm of the lobby was shattered. Out of the New York nowhere, a whirlwind of chaos erupted through the inconspicuous doors. A beautiful young woman, looking no older than 22, burst into the space, clutching a wailing toddler to her chest. Her hair was a mess, her makeup slightly smudged, and her eyes wild with panic and frustration.

Natasha's reaction was immediate. Her smile strained, muscles in her jaw tightening visibly as she hissed, "Maddie! Seriously? On time, and no kids! We talked about this. How could you bring Andrew?"

Andrew. Leah's toxic old colleague had that name. Ugh.

Maddie, her eyes welling up with tears of frustration and embarrassment, stammered out her explanation. "His dad canceled again, Tasha! And I couldn't afford a sitter... I didn't know what else to do." She paused. "Natasha, I couldn't miss tonight, not after everything..."

Her voice trailed off, choked with emotion. The toddler, sensing his mother's distress, wailed louder, his little face scrunched up in a perfect storm of toddler angst.

Leah and Mel watched the scene unfold, feeling like outsiders witnessing a family drama. Mel's discomfort was palpable, her body language screaming her desire to be anywhere but here. Leah, on the other hand, felt a surge of sympathy for the young mother. She remembered all too well the challenges of single parenthood, the constant juggling act, and the feeling of never quite measuring up.

To everyone's surprise, Natasha's demeanor suddenly softened. The hard edges of irritation melted away, replaced by a gentleness that seemed at odds with her usual brash persona. "Alright, kid," she said, her voice low and soothing. "You're still a MIILFF. Let's go."

She reached out, gently rubbing the toddler's back. "Hey there, little man. What's got you all worked up, huh?" Her touch and tone seemed to have a magical effect on the child, his wails subsiding to sniffles.

Maddie looked at Natasha gratefully, relief washing over her features. "Thank you, Tasha. I promise it won't happen again. I'll figure something out for next time."

Natasha waved off her apologies. "We'll deal with it. For now, let's just get you two inside before Mr. Grumpy Pants here decides to start a new concert."

With that, she led the now-expanded group toward a small but elegant hallway. The décor here was a stark contrast to the bland lobby – rich, dark wood paneling lined the walls, interspersed with abstract art pieces that hinted at sensuality without being overtly erotic. The lighting was soft and warm, creating an intimate atmosphere that was a world away from the harsh fluorescents of the entrance.

At the end of the hallway stood a private, discreet elevator. Its doors were a burnished gold, reflecting the warm light in a way that made them seem to glow from within. Natasha reached out to press the call button, her red-lacquered nail a stark contrast against the metallic surface.

Before she had a chance to make contact, however, the doors abruptly slid open. What emerged could only be described as an avalanche of humanity – four women poured out of the elevator in a tangle of limbs and raised voices.

"Natasha!"

The exclamation came from a well-dressed middle-aged woman in a lab coat. Her neon purple glasses sat askew on her nose, and her messy bun looked as if it had been subjected to a particularly vigorous about of hair-pulling. She was being escorted – or more accurately, manhandled – by the other three women, who gripped her shoulders firmly as they nudged her towards the lobby.

"Natasha! Are you ignoring me? It's Sorele!" The woman's voice rose in pitch, a note of hysteria creeping in. Her eyes, wide and slightly unfocused, darted around wildly before locking onto Natasha's face. "You! All of you! Monsters and Liars! LIARS!"

The scene was surreal, like something out of an avant-garde theater production. Leah and Mel stood frozen, unsure whether to intervene or run for the hills. Maddie clutched her son closer, turning slightly to shield him from the commotion.

Natasha, for her part, maintained an air of cool detachment. Her eyes flicked over the group, confusion and avoidance warring in her expression. With a swift motion, she ushered Leah, Mel, and Maddie into the now-empty elevator.

As the doors began to close, Natasha leaned in close, her voice a conspiratorial whisper. "I don't know who that crazy woman is," she said, her breath warm against their ears. "But she is unhinged, am I right? Shouting like a nutty person!"

The elevator doors sealed shut, cutting off the continued shouts from the lobby. In the sudden quiet, the soft ding of the elevator starting its ascent seemed unnaturally loud.

Natasha, seemingly unfazed by the bizarre encounter, turned her attention to Maddie's toddler. She bopped him playfully on the nose, her smile warm and genuine. "Here, cutie," she cooed, pulling a piece of gum from her purse. "A piece of gum so you can blow your own bubbles."

The little boy, his earlier tantrum forgotten, looked at the offered treat with shy curiosity. His mother, Maddie, smiled encouragingly. "Say thank you to Auntie Tasha, Andrew," she prompted gently.

Andrew reached out with a chubby hand, taking the gum with a quiet, "Thanks."

The elevator ride continued in tense silence. Mel's eyes darted around the small space, mentally cataloging possible escape routes. It was a habit she'd developed years ago, a remnant of a childhood spent moving from place to place, never quite feeling safe. Just in case, she thought. You never know.

Leah, in stark contrast to Mel's nervous energy, was practically bouncing on her toes with excitement. She chattered away, her words tumbling out in a stream of consciousness. "This is so exciting! I mean, did you see that lobby? And that woman in the lab coat – do you think she's part of the club? Oh, and Natasha, your outfit is amazing. Do you think they'll have drinks up there? I could use another coffee or maybe something stronger. What do you think we'll find? Is it like a secret society? Oh my god, what if it's some kind of fight club situation?"

Natasha listened to Leah's excited rambling with an indulgent smile, occasionally nodding or making sounds of agreement. Mel, for her part, seemed to withdraw further into herself with each passing second, her earlier misgivings clearly intensifying.

Finally, after what felt like an eternity but was likely only a minute or two, the elevator slowed to a stop. There was a moment of weighted silence as everyone held their breath, waiting for the doors to open and reveal whatever lay beyond.

Chapter Four
Heeling

With a soft chime, the elevator doors slid open, revealing a short hallway that ended in a set of large, frosted glass doors. The glass was etched with an intricate pattern that seemed to shift and change as they approached, never quite resolving into a recognizable image.

Natasha stepped out first, her heels clicking against the polished floor. She turned to face the group, her expression a mixture of excitement and mischief. With a flourish worthy of a stage magician, she gestured towards the frosted doors.

"MILFs," she sang out, her voice rich with anticipation, "Welcome to CLUB MIILFF!"

As if on cue, the frosted doors swung open, revealing the space beyond. The first impression was one of sensory overload – a kaleidoscope of colors, sounds, and scents that seemed to defy description.

The main room was vast, easily the size of a ballroom, with a ceiling that soared at least twenty feet high. Chandeliers dripping with crystals cast a warm, golden glow over the space, their light reflecting off mirrored surfaces scattered throughout the room. The walls were a deep, rich red, adorned with oversized art pieces that ranged from classic nudes to abstract expressionist works that hinted at the female form.

Scattered throughout the space were various seating areas – plush velvet couches, intimate booths with high backs for privacy, and even a few suspended egg chairs that looked like something out of a 60s sci-fi film. Each area was its own little oasis, some occupied by women engaged in animated conversation, others empty and inviting.

To the left, a long bar stretched along one wall, its surface a gleaming black marble shot through with veins of gold. Behind it, bartenders in crisp white shirts and black bow ties mixed drinks with a flair that bordered on performance art. The back wall of the bar was a floor-to-ceiling display of bottles, glass, and liquid, catching and refracting the light in mesmerizing patterns. The air was thick with the scent of perfume, alcohol, and something else – an undercurrent of excitement and possibility that seemed to hum through the room.

To the right, a stage dominated the space. Currently empty, its polished surface gleamed under the spotlight, promising entertainment to come. Plush velvet curtains in deep burgundy framed the stage, adding an air of mystery and anticipation.

As they took in the spectacle before them, each woman's reaction was distinct and telling.

Leah's eyes were wide with wonder, her earlier excitement now tinged with a hint of overwhelm. She'd never seen anything like this before – not in her sheltered upbringing, and certainly not in her life as a single mother. It was as if she'd stepped into another world, one where the rules she'd known all her life no longer applied.

"Oh my god," she breathed, her voice barely audible over the ambient noise of the club. "This is... it's..."

"Overwhelming?" Mel supplied her own expression, which was a mixture of awe and apprehension. Unlike Leah, Mel had seen her fair share of exclusive clubs and parties during her time in the entertainment industry. But this... this was something else entirely.

Natasha watched their reactions with undisguised glee, clearly enjoying their amazement. "Ladies," she purred, "welcome to your new playground."

Maddie, still holding Andrew close, looked around with a familiarity that spoke of previous visits. "Is the nursery still in the same place, Tasha?" she asked, bouncing her son gently as he started to fuss again.

Natasha nodded, pointing towards a discreet door near the back of the room. "Same spot, honey. Cookies on duty tonight – she'll take good care of our little man."

Leah's eyebrows shot up. "There's a nursery? In a club?"

Natasha laughed, a rich, throaty sound that drew admiring glances from nearby patrons. "Oh, sweetie. This isn't just any club. We're all about supporting each other – in every way possible. And Cookie is the best baby nurse this side of Brooklyn has ever seen."

As Maddie made her way to the nursery, Natasha led Leah and Mel deeper into the club. As they walked, heads turned to follow their progress. Leah felt a flush creep up her neck, unused to such open admiration. Mel, on the other hand, seemed oblivious to the attention, her eyes darting around, taking in every detail.

They approached a circular booth near the stage, its high back offering a degree of privacy while still allowing a view of the room. As they slid into the plush seats, a waitress materialized as if by magic.

"Welcome to Club MIILFF," she said, her smile warm and inviting. "What can I get for you ladies tonight?"

Before either Leah or Mel could respond, Natasha took charge. "We'll start with a round of the house special," she declared. "And some water for my friends here – they're going to need to stay hydrated."

As the waitress nodded and glided away, Mel fixed Natasha with a questioning look. "House special? Should I be worried?"

Natasha's laugh tinkled like ice in a glass. "Only if you're afraid of a good time, writer girl. Now, let's get down to business. You two are probably wondering what exactly you've gotten yourselves into, am I right?"

Leah nodded eagerly while Mel offered a more restrained, "The thought had crossed my mind, yes."

Leah added, "I still wanna know what the extra I and F stand for."

"Patience!" Natasha began, leaning in conspiratorially, "Club MIILFF is more than just a social club. We're a sisterhood, a support network, and yes, sometimes a little bit of a naughty escape from the daily grind of motherhood and life's responsibilities."

She paused as the waitress returned with their drinks – tall, elegant glasses filled with a shimmering, opalescent liquid that seemed to change color as it caught the light.

"But most importantly," Natasha continued, raising her glass in a toast, "we're about empowerment. Every woman here has a story, a struggle, a triumph. We celebrate it all."

Leah lifted her glass, the excitement evident in her eyes. "To empowerment," she echoed, taking a sip of the mysterious cocktail. Her eyes widened as the flavors exploded on her tongue – sweet, tart, with a hint of something exotic she couldn't quite place.

Mel, more hesitant, sniffed her drink before taking a small sip. Despite her reservations, she couldn't help but be impressed by the complex flavor profile. "This is... actually really good," she admitted.

As they sipped their drinks, Natasha began to explain more about the club's activities. "We have guest speakers, workshops on everything from finance to fitness, networking events, and, of course, our legendary parties."

She gestured towards the stage. "Tonight, we have a special treat. Dr. Eliza Sharma, a renowned psychologist specializing in women's issues, will be giving a talk on rediscovering your identity after motherhood."

Leah perked up at this. "That sounds fascinating! I've been struggling with that very issue since Jack left for college."

Mel, despite her initial skepticism, found herself intrigued. "I'm not a mother, but I can see how that would be a challenge. Dedicating so much of your life to raising a child, and then suddenly having to redefine yourself..."

Natasha nodded approvingly. "Exactly. And that's why you're here too, Mel. You might not be a mother in the traditional sense, but you're a creator. Your characters, your stories – they're your babies. And I bet you sometimes struggle with balancing your identity as a writer with the rest of your life, am I right?"

Mel blinked, surprised by Natasha's insight. "I... yeah, actually. That's spot on."

As they continued to chat, the club around them hummed with energy. Women of all ages, sizes, and backgrounds mingled freely, their laughter and conversation creating a warm backdrop to the evening.

Suddenly, the lights dimmed slightly, and a spotlight illuminated the stage. A hush fell over the crowd as a woman stepped into the light. Dr. Eliza Sharma was a striking figure – tall, with sleek black hair and sharp, intelligent eyes that seemed to take in the entire room at once.

"Good evening, ladies," she began, her voice rich and confident. "Tonight, we're going to talk about a journey. A journey of rediscovery, of reinvention, of reconnecting with the woman you were before you became 'Mom'..."

As Dr. Sharma launched into her talk, Leah found herself hanging on every word. It was as if the psychologist was speaking directly to her, addressing the very fears and insecurities she'd been grappling with since her child left for university.

Mel, too, was captivated, finding unexpected parallels between the challenges of motherhood and her own struggles as a writer. The idea of losing oneself in a role – be it parent or creator – and then having to redefine your identity resonated deeply.

Natasha watched her two companions with a satisfied smile, pleased to see them so engaged. This was what Club MIILFF was all about – creating connections, fostering understanding, and empowering women to embrace all aspects of their identities.

As the talk progressed, Leah found herself blinking back tears. Dr. Sharma's words had struck a chord, bringing to the surface emotions she'd been trying to ignore for months.

"It's okay to miss your child," Dr. Sharma was saying. "It's okay to feel a bit lost, to wonder who you are now that your primary role has shifted. But remember – you are more than just a mother. You always have been. Now is your time to rediscover all the other amazing facets of your identity."

Mel, noticing Leah's emotional response, reached out and gave her hand a gentle squeeze. It was a small gesture, but in that moment, it meant the world to Leah. Here she was, in this strange new environment, feeling more seen and understood than she had in years.

As Dr. Sharma's talk came to an end, the club erupted in applause. Women stood, cheering and wiping away tears, their faces alight with newfound determination and hope.

"So," Natasha said, turning to Leah and Mel as the applause died down, "what did you think of your first taste of Club MIILFF?"

Leah, her eyes shining, could barely contain her enthusiasm. "It's incredible! I've never felt so... understood. So, supported. Wait, what do you mean first?"

Natasha nodded, her smile warm and genuine. "Oh. There's more. We have our fun too – you should see our dance nights!" She winked mischievously. "But at our core, we're about empowerment and sisterhood."

Mel, her initial skepticism all but forgotten, found herself nodding along. "I have to admit, I'm impressed. When you first mentioned a club called MIILFF, I thought..."

"You thought it was going to be some sleazy pickup joint?" Natasha finished, laughing. "Don't worry, you're not the first. We like to play with expectations. Keep people on their toes."

As they continued to chat, the energy in the club shifted. The lights dimmed further, and music began to pulse through the room. Women moved towards the dance floor, their movements free and uninhibited.

"And now," Natasha announced, standing up and offering her hands to Leah and Mel, "it's time for the real fun to begin. Who's ready to dance?"

Leah, caught up in the moment and feeling more alive than she had in years, didn't hesitate. She grabbed Natasha's hand and stood, already swaying to the beat.

Mel hesitated for a moment, old insecurities bubbling to the surface. But as she looked around at the women on the dance floor – women of all shapes, sizes, and ages, all moving with joy and abandon – she felt something shift inside her.

"You know what?" she said, taking Natasha's other hand and standing up. "I think I am ready."

As they made their way to the dance floor, Leah caught Mel's eye. They shared a smile, an unspoken acknowledgment of the unexpected journey that had led them here. From a bizarre POGA class to this empowering, vibrant community – it had been quite a ride.

The night was still young, and as they began to dance, both women felt a sense of excitement for what was yet to come. Club MIILFF had opened the door to a world they never knew existed, a world of support, understanding, and yes, a little bit of mischief.

As the music pulsed around them and the energy of the club swept them up, Leah and Mel realized that their adventure was just beginning. And for the first time in a long time, they were both eager to see where it would lead.

"You ladies ready?" Natasha interrupted them. "Let's go see what's waiting for you inside."

With that tantalizing promise, she led them deeper into the heart of Club MIILFF, where secrets, empowerment, and unexpected alliances awaited. Little did Leah and Mel know their lives were about to change in ways they could never have imagined.

Chapter Five
Corporate Caffeine

Get up off the floor again
Gimme some peace, I fall to my knees.
I'm praying for Past beliefs, I catch and release, Betraying Dreaming so
deep, but I never sleep.
As you're writing this you didn't even sleep well last night
You see the signs and you're totally ignoring them
You talk about listening to your body.
Are you listening to your body?
Well, *you finally ate like a mensch today.*
You are going to need a good night of sleep. Is that clear? Caffeine.

Leah was not prepared for the breathtaking sight that greeted her as they stepped through the doors. Her eyes widened, drinking in every detail of the opulent space before her.

"Classy," she whispered, almost to herself. "Very classy."

The office – if you could call it that – was a marvel of modern design and luxury. Chandeliers dripping with high-end crystals cast an iridescent glow over Herman Miller workstations, each equipped with a personal espresso machine that gleamed like jewelry. Large white inflatable Pilates balls strategically replaced boring chairs, their presence both whimsical and practical.

Potted orchids, their delicate blooms, a stark contrast to the sleek lines of the furniture, and accented corners with touches of natural beauty. Cleverly placed stark white Bond Number 9 candles added to the ambiance, their subtle scent mingling with the unmistakable aroma of corporate ambition – a fragrance potent enough to fuel a Fortune 500 company.

This wasn't just an office; it was a living, breathing testament to high-octane fabulousness, where power plays were accessorized with stilettos, and billion-dollar deals were sealed with Montblanc pens. This wasn't just an office; this was a billionaire's playground.

Mel, standing beside Leah, let out a low whistle. "Well," she murmured, her writer's mind already spinning with descriptive phrases, "I think we've definitely left Kansas, Toto."

Leah turned to her new friend, a grin spreading across her face. "You can say that again. I feel like I've stepped into an episode of 'Lifestyles of the Rich and Famous'."

Before Mel could respond, a new voice boomed behind them, accompanied by the authoritative pitter-patter of kitten heels taking quick steps in their direction.

"Don't be fooled by those ridiculous Pilates Balls! I personally use a normal desk chair with a nice sturdy back!"

The women turned to see a short woman approaching, her presence somehow filling the vast space. Despite her diminutive stature, she exuded what could only be described as 5'11" energy. Her fur jacket, string of pearls, heavy Italian/ Brooklyn accent, and dark, glossy black hair reminded Leah of a character she had watched on Netflix, but the character's name evaded her at that moment.

The woman continued, her voice carrying a mix of authority and self-deprecating humor. "Personally, my 51-year-old saggy tush needs way more cushion than those measly balls can handle."

Natasha, who had been quietly observing the newcomers' reactions, burst into laughter. "Measly balls," she repeated, her eyes twinkling with mischief. "That's what I'm going to nickname my ex-husband." She took a deep drag from her kiwi-strawberry-flavored vape, blowing a large ball of smoke into the air.

Turning to the group, Natasha made introductions. "Krystal, this is Mel, Leah, and Maddie." She then bent down towards Andrew, her voice softening as she addressed the child. "And this little guy is Andrew. Andrew, say goodbye to Mommy for a bit. Wanna come with Auntie Tasha? We have a new fun video game room I can show you!"

Andrew's eyes widened with excitement, and he turned to his mother, silently pleading for permission. Maddie nodded her assent, a mix of relief and gratitude crossing her face.

"Ladies," Natasha continued, taking Andrew's pudgy hand in her own, "This is Krystal with a K. Last name Kream. Also, with a K. No, that's not her actual name, but that's what she goes by, and around here, we show respect. Even when people pick ridiculous nicknames."

Krystal rolled her eyes dramatically. "Around here we show respect," she mimicked, her tone playful but with an edge of annoyance. "And yet, you continue to blow smoke directly in my face." She pointed bluntly at the no-smoking sign above her and muttered, "Respect, my TUSH!"

Natasha, never one to back down, quipped back. "That sign says no smoking. This is a vape. Change the sign, and I'll change my behavior. Capisce?" To emphasize her point, she took another long drag before disappearing down a hall, Andrew scurrying behind her, waving goodbye to his mother.

As the sound of Natasha's heels and Andrew's excited chatter faded, Leah's attention snapped back to Krystal. Something had clicked in her mind, and her eyes widened in recognition.

"Wait a second!" Leah exclaimed, her voice rising with excitement. "Krystal Kream? As in the famous jewelry brand?" She waved her wrist, displaying a delicate bracelet. "I'm wearing one of their bracelets right now!"

Krystal winked, her heavily made-up face breaking into a grin that was equal parts pride and bitterness. She was a walking, talking caricature with cheeks that seemed perpetually flushed and blue eyeshadow that sparkled under the chandeliers' light. The character Leah thought about earlier came to life in the form of Krystal Kream.

If Susie Myerson from The Marvelous Mrs. Maisel and Joan Rivers had a love child, Krystal Kream would be it!

"Yep! That was my company," Krystal replied, her tone a complex mix of pride and resentment. She launched into her story, her hands moving animatedly as she spoke. "I started that business in the '80s with my own two hands, back when my identical twins were babies. I simply needed a simple way to tell those two apart! Hello? Identical twins!"

Leah and Mel exchanged glances, both captivated by Krystal's larger-than-life personality and her tale of entrepreneurial spirit.

"So," Krystal continued, "I ordered some tiny Swarovski's and other tchotchkes, and created two cute homemade name bracelets. Then, my neighbor saw the bracelets, asked me to custom design a few pieces, and the next thing I knew, the whole neighborhood was custom ordering from me. Different colors, designs... So, I did what nobody was doing. I sold the bracelets on Amazon, built the business, and hired a couple of workers to fulfill custom orders, and my bracelets were selling like hotcakes! I ran a tight ship!"

Leah was genuinely impressed. "That's... that's amazing," she said, grabbing Mel's shoulder and giving her an excited squeeze. Mel nodded in agreement, her writer's mind already spinning possible storylines inspired by Krystal's journey.

Krystal's expression darkened slightly. "Well, it was amazing," she said, her laugh tinged with sarcasm. "Until one day, I woke up and my Amazon account was suspended. Apparently, if you have a popular product and sell well, Amazon can copy your styles and sell them for cheaper. I couldn't compete. They were outsourcing labor, had million-dollar advertising campaigns, and bottom line, I was left with Bubkis. Nada. Zilch."

Mel's face softened with empathy. "That sucks," she said simply, understanding all too well the pain of having one's creative work undermined or stolen.

Krystal shrugged, her resilience shining through. "Eh, water under the bridge. I'm a MIILFF now. And trust me, kids, I'm doing fine." She leaned in conspiratorially, her voice dropping to a stage whisper. "See those chandeliers?"

Leah chuckled, glancing up at the sparkling fixtures. "They're kind of hard to miss."

"Those are my designs. Original Krystal Kream. And my chandeliers sell exclusively at high-end locations. Trust me, ladies, MIILFFs can do anything."

There was a moment of silence as the women absorbed Krystal's words and the implications behind them. Leah felt a surge of admiration for this woman who had faced setbacks and reinvented herself. Mel, despite her initial skepticism, found herself intrigued by the possibilities Krystal's story hinted at.

Chapter Six
MILK

The large green and white sign blazed through the steam rising from lattes clutched in manicured hands. The coffee shop sign hung above them, bold and unapologetic: MIILFBUCK$. The aroma of roasted coffee mingled with the sweet tang of ambition, creating an intoxicating atmosphere that seemed to pulse with possibility.

Krystal click-clacked her kitten heels with the practiced ease of a seasoned tour guide, leading the group through the bustling space. She paused, turning to face them with a flourish, and handed each of them a steaming cup of coffee.

Leah, ever the coffee addict, immediately began sipping. "Caffeine! Yes!" she exclaimed, her eyes lighting up with caffeinated joy.

Krystal's lips curved into a mischievous smile. " And now, for real, Welcome to Club MIILFF," she declared, a glint in her eyes, **"Mothers Interested in Launching Financial Freedom."**

The reaction was instantaneous. Frothy cappuccino threatened to erupt from Leah's nose. "Launching what?" she sputtered, eyes darting between the giggling barista and the sleek, silver plaque spelling out the acronym boldly.

"Financial freedom," Natasha drawled, a hint of amusement in her voice. "Don't let the name MILF fool you, toots. It stands for something much more... empowering."

Mel raised an eyebrow, her journalist's skepticism evident. "Really? Because it seems like you're trying awfully hard to make that acronym work."

Natasha shrugged, unperturbed. "Hey, if it gets attention and brings in the right people, who are we to argue with success, toots?"

"But seriously," Leah interjected, wiping foam from her upper lip, "how did you come up with this concept?"

Krystal's eyes twinkled. "Oh honey, necessity is the mother of invention. And when you've got a bunch of motivated mamas, well... let's just say the ideas start flowing faster than a leaky sippy cup."

As they moved past the coffee shop and into the expansive hallway beyond, a bustling ecosystem of female entrepreneurship revealed itself. Women were everywhere, engaged in various activities that radiated purpose and ambition. Some were on phones, voices animated as they discussed business deals. Others were hunched over tablets, fingers flying as they crunched numbers or drafted proposals. The energy in the air was palpable, a heady mix of determination and success.

Almost as if it was an afterthought, Krystal turned around coyly. "Here!" she said as she opened an app on her tablet with her pointer finger and held out her stylus pen with her other hand, "Need your signatures before you walk in..." Her eyes rolled to the office door. "There," her voice lowered. "They're NDAs—Non-Disclosure Agreements. Proprietary stuff in there, ya know!"

Leah and Maddie eagerly scribbled, as Mel lingered, gripping the stylus harder.

Leah's blue eyes implored Mel. *Come on Take a risk.*

Mel signed abruptly.

"Good call," smiled Leah.

Krystal led them to a small office door on the right and knocked twice. The door opened to reveal Meryl Dunaway, a vision of silver hair and steely resolve. She donned a simple black Prada suit and minimal makeup, her natural beauty needing little enhancement. Her presence commanded attention, and even Mel found herself straightening her posture instinctively.

"Welcome to Club MIILFF," Meryl said, her voice warm as she offered hugs to each of them. There was something in her manner that put them at ease despite her obvious power and influence. Was it her cheekbones? Her effortless warmth?

Krystal touched Meryl's hand with respect and affection. "This is the founder and president of Club MIILFF, ladies. Some of you may know her ex-husband, Barry Arthur Dunaway?"

Mel let out a squeal, her usual composure momentarily forgotten. "As in, Barry Arthur Dunaway, the producer of, like every incredible film I have ever watched?"

Meryl chuckled, a tinge of a British accent coloring her words despite her American roots. "The very one! I take it you're a fan."

Mel smiled sheepishly, suddenly aware of her outburst. "Sorta. I mean," she quickly backpedaled, "I know you said he's your ex, so..."

Meryl cut her off reassuringly. "Ex-husband because he traded me in for a younger model, and I traded him in for my Malibu Mansion. We're still friends, and I am still a fan of his work. But now," she smiled, a hint of satisfaction in her eyes, "I'm wealthier than him, and frankly, that feels really good." She laughed, the sound rich and genuine. "Plus, of course, we created the most beautiful project together." Her smile softened. "My daughter Ivanka, who is actually the vice president of Club MIILFF."

She motioned for them to follow. "Walk with me, let's see if she's free to say hi." As they walked, Meryl continued talking, her elegant steps matching the cadence of her words. "I'd like to think we're doing something powerful here, Ivanka and I. We took the word MIILFF and reclaimed it. The Queers have done it successfully. You're all too young to remember when using the word queer was an insult, and today... well, today people will tell you they're queer before you even ask."

Maddie, who had been quiet until now, piped up. "I have had the opposite experience. Andrew's Dad cheated on me with a much older woman." She lowered her voice to a whisper. "I think she was like... in her thirties!"

Natasha's eyes bulged, and she let out a dramatic gasp. "Oh really, toots? Thirties are much older? A few of us here are well in the 40-plus club, you better watch it." She puffed on her vape, sending a cloud of strawberry-scented vapor into the air.

Maddie blushed, realizing her faux pas. "Sorry..." she mumbled. "I meant... older than me."

"Everyone's older than you, Maddie. You're 22. And hot," Natasha said, moving towards Maddie compassionately. "You'll be fine!" She paused, turning to Meryl. "Meryl, tell her she'll be fine."

Meryl smiled, her eyes kind but determined. "You will be fine," she assured Maddie. Her lips pursed thoughtfully. "In fact, you will be more than fine once you have your own financial freedom." She adjusted her hair and continued. "You see, people underestimate what it takes to build wealth. I have met too many mothers with real talent. Writers, doctors, researchers, artists, creatives, business people --" She paused and repeated, emphasizing each word, "Real brains and real talent. And too many times, I have witnessed them suffering along year after year, trying to get resources. Finally, if they do get access to resources, they don't have the proper training or access to use those resources effectively, and then," she paused, her voice tinged with sadness, "They become stuck. Stuck in a world where they deeply desire financial freedom but just can't seem to get there."

She waved her hands passionately as she spoke, her energy infectious. "Here at CLUB MIILFF, we remove all the bottlenecks. When a fellow MIILFF has an idea, we listen, and we learn. We see how we can support her vision, and we make it happen. Through hard work, we have built endless connections in every industry. And the best part, it always comes back to the MIILFF. Lawyers, publicists, dancers, social media management, finance, small business operators, high-end escorts, patenting, licensing, selling, executives, purchasing, creating, networking!" She paused for effect, her almost British accent taking center stage. "These aren't just buzzwords. We put our money where our mouth is."

Leah's eyes widened. "High-end escorts? That's... quite a range of services."

Meryl's smile didn't falter. "We support all forms of entrepreneurship, darling. No judgment here."

As they reached another office door, Meryl stopped, her demeanor shifting slightly. She knocked twice, her voice taking on a sing-song quality. "Ivanka darling, do you have a minute to meet some potential members? They're just visiting today!"

"Come, come!" Ivanka's voice called from inside. As they entered, they saw a striking young woman gesturing for them to join her while she finished a phone call. "Sorry," she whispered, "I'll be done in a minute."

Turning her attention back to the phone conversation, Ivanka's voice took on a more authoritative tone. "Listen, Reese, you and I both know the buyout's going to happen sooner or later, so my suggestion is, sell while it's hot and don't wait for the merger." She paused to take a sip from her simple thermos. "Great, I'll have my assistant send you the paperwork!"

She hung up, exhaled sharply, took a sip of her celery smoothie, and smiled wide. "Hi!"

Meryl beamed with pride as she turned to the group. "Ivanka is one of CLUB MIILFF's lawyers. She represents some of our talent here. Beauty and brains."

Ivanka sprinted from her chair to the door, her energy palpable. "Honestly, guys, I love what I do, and the best part? As an actual MILF (I have a 7-year-old), my favorite part of CLUB MIILFF is the work-life balance. I only come in twice a week and get to do all the things I prefer doing! Like traveling with my husband Mark (we'll be celebrating our 9th anniversary next week), picking my daughter up from school every day…"

"Not every day," interrupted Meryl, her eyes lighting up. "Wednesdays are carpool days for Grandma!"

They shared a laugh, and the warmth between mother and daughter was evident.

Maddie stepped forward, extending her hand. "Hi, I'm Maddie, Natasha's sister."

Ivanka smiled warmly, clasping Maddie's hand in both of hers. "Maddie! Finally! Natasha has been telling us about you since your baby was born. You know something, I think you may be our youngest MILF here, Maddie. And I'd love to talk to you about potentially overseeing our under-21 Club. It's still in the development stages, but we would love to have your input. Some too many young mothers are being robbed of bright futures. I want to set them up for success, and Gen Z is a target we haven't even touched on yet. I'm sure they have so many contributions and ideas." She looked at Maddie earnestly. "I hope we can partner on this. I really want your voice on this project!"

Maddie looked both intimidated and flattered, her eyes wide with the possibilities Ivanka was presenting. "I… always wanted to open my own nursing school. My mom was a nurse, and she always had flexibility."

Leah was hooked. Not only was this woman beautiful, but she was intelligent and kind. She found herself imagining what it would be like to work alongside someone like Ivanka, to be part of something so empowering and revolutionary.

Even Mel, usually the skeptic of the group, was impressed. "I gotta say, when I saw the invite, I was gonna pass. Based on, you know. The name." She laughed shyly. "But you two are really inspiring."

Krystal turned to Natasha, a mock pout on her face. "Notice how she said 'you two' and left us out of it."

Natasha cracked her gum. "Noticed. And noted."

Mel laughed, realizing her oversight. "Guys, you are too! Seriously. This is all really inspiring."

Meryl's gaze turned serious as she exchanged a knowing glance with Natasha. "Natasha, they've been inspired. I think they're ready to be awed." She pronounced each syllable carefully, building anticipation.

Meryl turned to face the woman, her demeanor both warm and professional. "MILFs, I leave you in good hands. My door is always open -- as long as you knock twice." She winked. "Hope to see you all again really soon. Perhaps at our monthly meeting?" She politely embraced them goodbye, as mother and daughter disappeared into Ivanka's office, leaving Krystal to continue the grand tour.

"Alright MILFs, let's keep walking!" Krystal ushered them down the expansive hallway and opened a door, revealing a sight that took their breath away.

"Whoa," breathed Maddie, her eyes wide with amazement. "This is seriously next-level wedding prep central!"

The ladies stepped into a magnificent, buzzing space. Laptops hummed, screens glowed with a kaleidoscope of wedding photos, and the very air seemed tinged with the sweet scent of honeysuckle.

"Welcome to I DO!" chirped Krystal, a proud grin splitting her face. "Let me introduce you to the diamond herself, Mimi."

A petite woman, vibrant and ageless, emerged from a cluster of assistants. "Hello, MILFs! I'm so glad you could make it." Despite her obvious success, there was a disarming warmth in her smile that put everyone at ease.

Mimi launched into her story with enthusiasm. "I used to plan weddings. And after my third runaway bride and enough cleanups in the industry, I set out to be a personal wedding concierge. Stepping in from the moment a client gets engaged up until the wedding night. I got to know my brides and grooms intimately, they shared their anxieties with me, and I learned to tap into therapists, friends, family members and gently nudge the couple back together. I ended up catching the attention of Oprah, who labeled me as the 'Pre-Marital-Marital Planner' and now, I run the largest wedding planning and couples counseling hub in the tri-state area." Her voice swelled with pride.

Leah couldn't contain her excitement. "This is literally like the Orbitz for brides! Genius."

Mimi beamed at the comparison. "Orbitz, but better. We've taken the stress out of wedding planning, and my entire staff behind the scenes have been in the wedding planning business for years! So, they spend their days creating packages, negotiating with vendors, and offering every kind of coaching to the couple, and sometimes, even the couple's families." She giggled. "You wouldn't even believe it. Now, I DO have a waiting list of the top talent in all the fashion, beauty, and wedding spheres begging us to be featured on our site. I mean, why not? They get guaranteed bookings and paid upfront. Everyone wins."

Mel was genuinely impressed. "That is insane!"

"I know!" Mimi agreed enthusiastically. "I basically had the idea but just didn't have the funding or resources. CLUB MIILFF is literally like Shark Tank, but for MILFs. With a much bigger network and way more money. And, well, here I am. Talk about financial freedom!"

"Sounds like a dream," Leah added, her mind already racing with possibilities.

"Damn right," Krystal affirmed, her voice buzzing with excitement. "And wait till you see the destination wedding feature in the new app they're building! Bora Bora, here I come." She paused, a hint of wistfulness in her voice. "The only thing I'm missing is a husband."

Leah couldn't resist a playful jab. "And none on the horizon, huh?"

Natasha snorted with laughter, but her expression quickly turned serious. "Jokes aside, Mimi's counseling business alone profited a cool three mill last quarter! And that's not even including the actual events!"

The women gasped, their faces glowing with admiration. Three million dollars in a single quarter, funded by the illustrious CLUB MIILFF? Mimi was way more than a planner; she was a business powerhouse, a testament to creativity and sheer grit. And her buzzing empire promised to revolutionize the world of weddings with the simple click of a button. What was most impressive to all the women was how this business was owned and operated by a MILF who turned a wedding business into an empire.

Leah whispered to Mel, unable to contain her awe. "Talk about an actual MILF..."

Mel nodded in agreement, a hint of a blush coloring her cheeks. "She is kinda hot," she gossiped back.

Krystal, overhearing their whispered exchange, nudged them along. "Lot's more to see here, MILFs. Let's keep it moving."

She waved her hand towards the corridor, leading them past more endless doors, each promising new wonders and possibilities. Behind one door, they entered a large room that could only be described as a pure fantasy for barbecue lovers.

Red and white checkered tablecloths adorned modern white picnic tables, while bustling women wearing chef's hats, lab coats, and aprons measured meat temperatures with scientific precision. Whimsical-looking slushie machines lined one wall, a quaint array of old-fashioned pickle barrel stands occupied another corner, and a full s'mores bar with every kind of topping imaginable beckoned from the far end of the room.

Natasha and Krystal wasted no time making a beeline for the freshly grilled pineapple samples. As they savored the sweet and smoky flavors, a middle-aged woman with frosted blonde tips that seemed frozen in time from the eighties approached them.

"It's a new recipe I'm trying for the new product line," Itta shared with them, her eyes twinkling with pride. Itta, slightly pale but exuding a warmth that made you instantly like her, was the mother of a son with autism. Just two short years ago, she had become the owner and chief operator of "Girl Grill," a multi-million-dollar barbecue brand designed for women by women.

"You can't spell grill without girl!" Itta quipped, her catchphrase clearly well-practiced but delivered with genuine enthusiasm. Her Australian accent was mesmerizing.

Leah, intrigued by the concept, couldn't help but ask, "How did you come up with this idea? It's brilliant!"

Itta's face lit up at the question, clearly eager to share her story. "Well, it all started with a simple problem at a neighbor's cookout," she began, settling into her tale. "Two summers ago, I was enjoying the party when my son started throwing a massive tantrum because there were separate ketchup and mustard bottles. He insisted that the ketchup bottle should just have two spouts with both options -

one for ketchup and one for mustard. He kicked, yelled, and screamed until I literally had no choice but to take him home."

She paused, her expression softening. "Raising a child with autism is difficult, but it also opens your eyes to possibilities you might never have considered otherwise."

Maddie nodded sympathetically, thinking of her own challenges as a young mother.

Itta continued her story, her excitement building. "When I got home, I started thinking -- is my kid onto something? Why shouldn't a bottle have multiple spouts? I gave it a shot. I custom made one bottle with four spouts." She lowered her voice conspiratorially, "Kind of like those old-fashioned pens that you can click! Remember how each click changed the pen's color? Except here, each pump of the spout changed the condiments - you can choose to dispense ketchup, mayo, mustard, and BBQ sauce depending on which spout you press -- all in one bottle!"

Mel and Leah nodded, flashing back to memories of those click pens. Maddie, too young to relate, listened with rapt attention, nonetheless.

"Anyways," Itta continued, her voice filled with wonder at her own success, "Apparently, I was onto something. Who knew? Meryl introduced me to someone she knew at the Home Shopping Network, and I ended up selling out my entire product in two days of filming! Two days! It was nuts! Before I knew it, magazines started blogging about me and invited me on their shows. They would introduce me as 'the woman who created a super cool condiment dispenser inspired by her son's sensory needs.'"

Her eyes shone with pride as she added, "Ivanka helped me patent my product, and then I started creating other cool grill products. Before I knew it, my one condiment dispenser creation parlayed into a multi-million-dollar empire: 'Girl Grill.' All thanks to CLUB MIILFF."

Mel was in awe, witnessing pure possibility unfold before her eyes. The writer was already spinning this into a potential story, seeing the narrative arc of a mother's love and innovation leading to unexpected success.

Maddie, clearly impressed, chimed in, "I've seen all your products in HomeGoods, and I drool every time!"

Itta beamed at the compliment. "Well, honey, remind me before you leave, and I'll make sure you go home with a Girl Grill starter kit. Every MILF should have one!"

As they prepared to move on, Leah couldn't resist asking one more question. "Itta, what's been the most rewarding part of this journey for you?"

Itta's eyes misted over slightly. "You know, it's not the money, although that's nice. It's not even seeing my products in stores, although that's a thrill. It's the letters I get from other parents of kids with special needs. They tell me how my products have made their lives easier, how they've been able to enjoy family barbecues without stress for the first time. That's what makes it all worthwhile."

The women nodded, touched by Itta's sincerity. As they left the Girl Grill area, each of them felt a renewed sense of possibility. If Martha could turn a family challenge into a million-dollar idea, what might they be capable of?

"Let's keep it moving, MIILFFs!" Krystal called, ushering them back into the hallway.

CHAPTER SEVEN
THE MIILFF MIDAS TOUCH

Stop paying attention to the things that make you tired
To the things that make you feel boring
But social media
But weed
But sugar
But focusing on other people
But… brand names
But my trauma
Stop Fighting the system
A new liberation
Comes from the silence
Within
I hate the silence
One day you will embrace the silence
Silence is elegant
Just Breathe

Each door Krystal opened revealed another testament to the club's Midas touch. They met renowned chefs, artists, and motivational speakers whose fees had tripled thanks to representation from the most sought-after NYC PR and Branding firm, "EDEM" - Every Day Extraordinary Moms.

Natasha, seeing the look of confusion on their faces, explained, "Jessica Altman, a brilliant single Mom with guts and chutzpah, founded EDEM. She approached Calvin Klein with a genius campaign idea: feature 1000 everyday extraordinary Moms in Calvin Kleins and release the campaign all at once on one day. Worldwide."

Mel's eyebrows shot up. "That's... ambitious. How did it go?"

Krystal grinned. "Each featured Mom was already a small micro-influencer with a minimum of 100,000 followers. Needless to say, the campaign went viral instantly. People loved the EDEM concept. Jessica was hailed as the 'most brilliant marketing genius of 2020.' Today, each mom originally featured in the Calvin Klein campaign commands a fat paycheck, and EDEM represents the top talent nationwide."

"Jessica Altman was quite the MIILFF," Natasha added with a wink.

Leah whistled, impressed. "Talk about leveraging influence. But how did they manage the logistics of such a massive campaign?"

Krystal's eyes twinkled. "Ah, that's where the MIILFF magic comes in. We pooled our resources, our connections. Every MIILFF pitched in - from tech gurus streamlining the process to PR mavens coordinating the rollout. It was a testament to what we can achieve when we work together."

As they continued their tour, they encountered a group of friends who had started the "Billion Dollar Book Club" -- a book club initiative that immediately placed their recommendations on bestseller lists and led to creative perks and high-priced exclusive membership fees.

Mel's journalistic instincts kicked in. "A book club that influences bestseller lists. Isn't that a bit... unethical?"

Natasha shrugged, taking a long drag from her vape. "Ethics, schematics. It's all about influence, baby. Besides, we're promoting literacy. That's gotta count for something, right?"

Leah kept pinching herself. This was real. The possibilities seemed endless, each new discovery more exciting than the last. She found herself imagining what kind of business she might start, what untapped potential she might have.

"You know," Leah mused, her mind racing, "I've always had this idea for a tech startup that combines cybersecurity with user-friendly interfaces. Something that makes online safety accessible to every-one, not just tech experts."

Krystal's eyes lit up. "Now that's what I'm talking about! Let's schedule a brainstorming session. We'll get you connected with our tech MIILFFs faster than you can say 'firewall.'"

As the tour concluded, they found themselves in the plush confines of the "Medical MILF Spa." The air hung heavy with the sweet scent of brewed cannabis tea and hushed whispers. Champagne flutes materialized as if by magic, meeting their lips with promises of luxury and indulgence.

Natasha, ever the enigma, smirked. "A little pre-massage indulgence, ladies. You deserve it after all this excitement."

Mel, her mind reeling from everything they'd seen, finally voiced the question that had been gnawing at her all day. "Natasha, what's the catch? This all seems too good to be true."

Leah, ever the optimist, chimed in, "Maybe they take a percentage of our success? I mean, think about it. I'd be happy to share a percentage if it means millions for me."

Natasha, a knowing smile playing on her lips, uttered a single, cryptic phrase: "A piece of the MILF pie, of course."

Before anyone could press for clarification, Krystal interrupted. "Ok, people. Listen up." She removed three electronic key fobs from her pocket, holding them up like precious artifacts. "Here's the deal. These are keys to CLUB MIILFF. They're temporary. These keys will only work for the next two weeks."

Maddie questioned, confusion evident in her voice, "Just two weeks?"

Natasha chided, lightly punching her sister's shoulder, "Let her finish!"

Krystal continued, her tone brooking no further interruptions, "Yeah, let me finish! So, for the next two weeks, you can come back as often as you like. Take tours, ask questions, speak to the MIILFFs," she flounced her hands dramatically. "Mi casa es su casa!" (Her heavy Italianism accent added an unnecessary but very necessary R: "Mi casar, su casar.")

"Basically," she went on, "see how we can help you gain financial freedom, use the spa if you want, come back for lattes, you name it. You have unlimited access to everyone and everything at CLUB MIILFF."

"And?" asked Leah, furrowing her barely-there brows. "What happens after two weeks?"

Krystal responded without missing a beat. "After two weeks, you make a decision. You either join the club and we set you up with your exclusive membership, or you pass, forget about us, and never forget you signed an NDA."

Mel, ever the journalist, couldn't help but probe further. "What does set us up for membership entail?"

Krystal made direct eye contact with Mel, her gaze intense. "You want all the answers now, don't you?"

Mel shrugged, unapologetic in her curiosity.

"The only expectation we have in two weeks is a business idea," Krystal explained. "If you want to be part of the club, you bring the idea. That's your ticket to membership. And believe me, you want these perks. Think about it - once you become a member, CLUB MIILFF will make your idea a reality. Whatever it takes."

Natasha turned to Mel and whispered, her voice low and enticing, "Remember when I told you that your screenplay can happen? Believe me," her voice dropped even lower, "it can happen."

The three friends found themselves standing in the hallway of possibilities, the MIILFBucks sign casting an ethereal glow on their faces. Mel, eyes narrowed with suspicion, replayed Natasha's words in her mind. It can happen. The promise was tempting, almost too good to be true, and yet...

Leah, her gaze fixed on the glittering cityscape visible through a nearby window, dreamt of financial freedom and the possibilities it held. "I just need a solid business idea," she murmured, more to herself than anyone else.

And Natasha, cloaked in an unspoken secret, remained a complex question, the enigmatic gatekeeper to a world of boundless potential and an undeniable sense of intrigue.

As they prepared to leave, each woman lost in her own thoughts, Krystal's voice cut through their reverie. "Remember, ladies, two weeks. Make them count."

The next two weeks would be a whirlwind of exploration and decision, a test of their ambition and a tantalizing glimpse into the world of CLUB MIILFF, where dreams came to fruition, fortunes were made, and the true meaning of a seemingly ordinary acronym remained shrouded in mystery. And money. Lots and lots of money.

CHAPTER EIGHT
BILLION-DOLLAR BRAINWAVES

Paper Lovin

If you can't love me now

Don't love me later

When my later is much greater

It only means that you love the paper…

All they ever wanted from her was money.

First, as a young bride, there were whispers between her parents.

"No one needs to know we have money struggles!"

Followed by, "Well, how are we going to pay for her Chasunah!"

It was Leah's Chasunah they couldn't afford. A wedding to a man she knew for a few short months. A wedding she didn't want to have.

She was 19, living in a home with a father who had beaten her since she was a baby, often until she was black and blue. Sometimes, her mother would "let" her stay home from school just because she had been covered in too many noticeable strap marks.

Her mother would look at her neck and say, "You need to stay home from school today." She pursed her lips tightly, "I mean, who knows what the school will think."

Little Leah understood.

In our community, this is what matters most: WHAT WILL PEOPLE THINK?

"I mean, it isn't really my fault that I get angry," her father would sheepishly grin, "I am a KOHEN. Everyone knows Kohanim (holy priests) have tempers."

Little Leah would nod. Nodding was better than crying. Crying led to further beatings.

"Now come give me a kiss," he would say.

A kiss

After he beat her, she would have to kiss his rageful, spitty, angry monster face.

She obliged with a kiss (In Yiddish, a kiss is called "pussy")> Often, her father would say, "Come here and gimme five puthies!" (He had a lisp)

As a young bride, weeks before her wedding, her parents notified Leah that due to the urgency of wedding planning and because the other side was taking too long to make decisions, her parents had decided to use her savings.

"Well," smiled her mom." Not all of it!"

Leah was in shock. She had worked for every dollar of those 41 thousand dollars since she was 14. She had tutored, directed productions, held multiple teaching positions, and saved every bit of Hanukkah money she ever received from Bobba Chaya. This was her hard-earned money! Her one shot at independence in the real world.

Her mother continued. "Since I originally opened the account with you, I was able to withdraw 38 thousand dollars. "

She paused.

"See, I even left you three thousand. That should be enough!"

Leah blinked.

"I need to pay for your sheitels. Do you know how expensive a custom wig is? Thousands! And you need a weekday one, and of course, a nicer one wig for Shabbos. Plus, you need fancy furniture. Anyway, you're getting married. In a month, you will have a husband, and then he will take care of you. So technically, you don't even need money."

Leah blinked.

Her husband did not take care of her. In fact, he made her work three jobs and drank the dollars away. She took extra work to pay for Disney trips, day camps, and high-end lessons for her boy. He was not just brilliant (high honors society). He was a wildly talented guitarist, and she was always saving for the finest coaches and top training programs. He would have the absolute best of everything life had to offer. She would see to it.

After years of her husband's drinking, lying, violence and unemployment, she gave him the ultimatum. "Get a job and get well or give me a divorce." Turns out asking for a get (Jewish divorce) from your husband, his Rabbi, parents, and community is more terrifying than asking your toxic boss for a much-deserved raise.

"I will never give you a divorce," he sneered. "Pay me, and maybe then, we can talk."

She took extra jobs and saved every penny. She was too ashamed to admit that her marriage was a failure and that her parents would never allow her to come back home.

He threatened. "If you ever want any custody of Jack, I am not giving you a dime. Do you think anyone in our community will support you once they know you're a lesbian? If you want to keep your freedom, pay me."

It always came down to the money.

And then, a few short years later, there was Svetlana. Beautiful, young, Russian, demanding, spoiled Svetlana. She and Leah bonded over traumas, and despite Svetlana being ten years younger than her - a smoker (nicotine, ew!) broke (really Leah) and emotionally unwell (poor girl had an abusive father and was severely abused by several supposed "mentors") Leah was hooked. Svetlana's family had loved her like a daughter, and treated Jack like one of the boys. Finally, Leah had the full family she so desperately craved. Plus, a beautiful woman who depended on her.

"If you don't give me my dream wedding, I will never be happy."

Her green eyes pierced Leah's soul.

Leah tried to reason with her. "Listen, Svetlana. I had a wedding already. It was lavish and expensive, and I can tell you that stuff really doesn't matter. What matters is what comes after the people are gone. Why should I waste my money on a one day event when we can save the money for a life together?"

Svetlana would sob, and Leah, as always, would cave.

Jack, ever the parentified only child, would often call his mom out on her utter oblivion, "Mom, why are you forcing yourself to do this? You don't even want a wedding!"

Leah was too ashamed to admit the ugly truth to her own child. If she didn't spend the money, Svetlana would be unhappy. And Leah needed to be the good guy. She needed to spend the money she really didn't have, so everyone would be "happy."

But why would you take my money to pay for a wedding I don't want?

Oh, Leah, Why would you pay for a wedding you didn't want?

Why would I let her leave me with nothing?

Leah wiped a tear that was heading towards her neck and interrupting her yoga flow.

Why do I always cry when I practice the Happy Baby?

I deas. She had hundreds. Leah had always been brimming with ideas. From a very young age, her entrepreneurial spirit shone brightly, even in the confines of her ultra-religious upbringing. During summers in the Catskills, she'd organize evening activities for the girls in her bungalow colony, charging a modest twenty-five cents per attendee. Her creativity knew no bounds--- concerts, sales, contests, productions, auctions---always two steps ahead of her peers and ready to take risks.

Her mother's words echoed in her memory: "You're too smart for your own good, Layla. Boys don't like such smart girls who take charge." She would pause and lower her voice. "You'll never snatch a husband like that."

Ironically, as it turned out, Leah preferred romantic relationships with women. It took nearly three decades for her to realize there was nothing "wrong" or "sinful" about her attraction to beautiful women. Even at 40, she grappled with imposter syndrome, feeling "too gay," "too progressive," or "not liberal enough," depending on her surroundings. Leah's surroundings ranged from in-the-closet religious friends, to no longer religious, to non-Jewish, to very religious and everyone in between. At some point, she stopped worrying about whose level she was at and started expecting her friends to meet her where she was. It was mutual and safe with most of her friends. But not her family.

Her family's rejection had been gradual but absolute. Declined calls became less frequent invitations, which evolved into silent treatment and finally, complete excommunication. Leah often quipped, "I experienced cancel culture before the cool kids invented it." Humor had always been her coping mechanism for navigating life's harsh realities.

Judaism was a journey for Leah, as she learned to rewrite new chapters in a book that was rife with religious trauma. Her parents were children of Holocaust survivors, and the scarcity mentality they were raised with left them ill-equipped to understand that there are many paths of "Yiddishkeit." Leah's upbringing included so many unwritten rules that were intended to add protection to a community terrified of being targeted, but instead, those rules became shackles to Leah, and as a non-conformist, Leah was learning that embracing those struggles along the way was indeed possible without shame, critique, and judgment.

She could still hear her mother's voice, "You're not wearing a sheitel and you think you can just march into shul like that?"

After Leah received her Get (lawful Jewish divorce), she uncovered her hair (a sin according to many Rabbis and Jewish law) and removed her wig, commonly referred to as a sheitel. To Leah, the wig felt oppressive, and although she had endless respect for the women who chose to cover their hair and follow Jewish law stringently, she had made peace with her own journey back to a truer Judaism. She would focus on re-learning slowly and integrate stringencies when she felt ready, without letting her Jewish guilt play into her authentic decision-making process. She would only focus on learning the traditions one at a time and slowly taking on more as she leveled up.

It was that exact thought process that led her to the Brooklyn Bay Synagogue. Her friend Shonna was close with the Rabbi, a mentor and family friend. Shonna insisted that Leah get her "tush" to shul just in time for an outdoor Kiddush.

Suddenly, a flash of movement across the aisle caught her eye. A woman, undeniably beautiful, devoured a plate of gefilte fish with an almost comical gusto. The woman's fitted black suit clung to every androgynous curve, somehow defying the messiness of the fish as she effortlessly scooped another bite. Loose black hair framed a face that seemed both striking and approachable. This woman was radiating confidence and an aura of quiet power.

"Shonna," Leah hissed, nudging her friend. "Who's the woman in the killer suit devouring the gefilte fish like there's no tomorrow?"

Shonna, a self-proclaimed "Jewish Yenta," lowered her voice conspiratorially. "That's Dr. Ris. Top cardiac surgeon at Mount Sinai. Sits on the medical board of half the pharmacies in the city. And get this. For fun, she hikes! And paints!"

Leah was interested. "Impressive. But is she single?"

Shonna's smile dimmed. "Leah, honey, you are not Rava's type. Not to mention, she's seeing someone."

Leah shrugged, a mischievous glint in her eyes. "The good ones always are." She shrugged again, accepting that Rava and her wouldn't be a romantic match. "I'm still going to invite her to join our outings. There aren't many Jewish lesbians our age who come to synagogue, the more, the merrier!"

While Leah might not have been the traditional "Rava type," there was something undeniably magnetic about Leah. People gravitated towards her light and positive personality. As soon as the service ended, Leah, with her usual extroverted charm, made a beeline for Rava.

"Hey, you!" Leah greeted with a grin that could light up a room. "Didn't know Mount Sinai doctors moonlighted as competitive eaters."

Rava, caught mid-conversation with another woman, turned, a surprised smile gracing her lips. Her eyes, a warm hazel, held a depth that immediately captivated Leah.

"Uh, hi there," Rava stammered, wiping a stray bit of fish from her finger. "I wouldn't call it competitive eating, more like a healthy appreciation for a childhood favorite."

The conversation flowed easily, a delightful mix of witty banter and heartfelt insights. Leah learned about Rava's demanding career, her surprisingly traditional upbringing despite her reform background, and her love for obscure 80s hair bands and most 80s movies (a point that scored major points with Leah mostly because she had missed out on so many cool movies growing up being completely restricted from movies, TV, and secular entertainment). Rava, in turn, discovered Leah's passion for social justice work, dancing, music jams, passion for cooking, surprisingly deep knowledge of Jewish mysticism, and her infectious laugh that could fill any silence.

"You should come for a hike with me some time," Rava offered.

Leah was excited, "I'm not a major hiker, but I'd love to learn!"

"Awesome, you pick a place for us to sleep over near the trail, and I'll bring gear!" Rava seemed excited too.

"Wait." Leah looked surprised. "There's gear?"

Rava laughed. "Oh boy, you're a real beginner, aren't you!"

As the group dispersed, Leah, ever the social butterfly, invited Rava to join her and her friends for an upcoming Pride event. Rava hesitated, a flicker of amusement dancing in her eyes.

"Pride, huh? I wouldn't exactly call myself..." she began, then stopped, a blush creeping up her neck.

Leah chuckled, "What? Are you embarrassed to say gay?"

It was that first conversation and the glimmer in Rava's eye, coupled with witty banter, lots of laughter, endless dates, and undeniable chemistry, that set the stage for their two-year relationship. Leah had finally found her best friend, and romance was the cherry on top.

On that Sunday afternoon, Leah snagged a reservation at Bonds, a trendy New York City sushi spot.

"This spicy tuna is insane!" Rava exclaimed, her eyes lighting up with each bite.

Leah loved the way Rava enjoyed food. It was sexy.

Leah smiled, peeling an edamame pod. "But can you believe Club MIILFF is legit? It seems too good to be true."

"Seems legit to me," Rava responded, fearlessly biting into a chunk of wasabi. "They fund unique businesses, and in return, they profit when you succeed. Not a bad concept."

Leah sighed heavily. "True. I guess I just have to come up with a great business idea."

Rava reached across the table, gently squeezing Leah's hand. "Leah, out of everyone I know, you're by far the best businessperson I've seen. Your employees respect you, your boss depends on you. You're great at negotiating. Remember last week when you helped me develop a marketing strategy for our concierge services in about ten minutes?"

Leah smiled sheepishly. "I remember. I just wish there was a way I could teach people how to run their own businesses instead of constantly working for others. In my twenties and thirties, I never really knew about budgeting. As a single mother, I spent everything I earned on my child---the best music lessons, expensive camps, lavish vacations. I climbed the corporate ladder on my own, with no connections and zero formal education."

She laughed, a hint of irony in her voice. "And in a world where my child can choose anything, they choose to identify as non-binary!"

Rava chuckled. "I think it's funny, and knowing your child, I think they would appreciate the humor too. Even if the joke is about their gender." She paused, her expression turning serious. "Now, for the real question---are we getting the crème brûlée or the hot fudge sundae?"

"Both," Leah declared without hesitation. Then, her eyes lit up with sudden inspiration. "You know, I really do want to teach people all over the world how to climb the corporate ladder. I did it despite every possible obstacle---an arranged marriage, missed education, no internships. But with intuition and tenacity, I made it. I bet there are millions of women like me craving career growth who would love tips and tricks on how to get there."

Rava leaned forward, recognizing the familiar spark in Leah's eyes. "Oh boy, you're getting that lightbulb look. Your face is scrunching up, and you're becoming really animated. I've seen this before---it means you're onto something!"

Leah nodded excitedly. "You know what? I think I am. I have a good business idea, Rava. It may be unconventional and a huge risk, but if anyone can help me get there, it's Club MIILFF." She lowered her voice to a whisper. "They have every resource someone could possibly dream of. I really think I have something here."

Rava grinned supportively. "See? I told you. But now, we have more pressing matters to attend to."

"Oh?" Leah blinked, puzzled.

Rava's eyes darted upward toward the server approaching with two dessert plates. "Yes, such as which dessert is better. It's time for a taste test."

Leah laughed and picked up her spoon. "Oh, this is very serious indeed."

As they dug into their desserts, the glimmer in Leah's eye sparkled brighter than ever. A new business idea, plus hot fudge? The future held nothing but promise.

CHAPTER NINE
THE CORPORATE MINUTE REVOLUTION

360
I went my own way, and I made it
I'm your favorite reference baby
Breathe Just breathe
Phy-Tra
Ouch
Ouch Ouch Ouch
Little Leah felt the pain
Grab
Squeeze
Blood
Ouch
Why would you kick me and punch me?
Why would I let it?
Slap across the face
Another slap across the face
I'm an adult now
I get to control this narrative.
Leah turned to Svetlana." Don't you ever touch me like that again?"
Huge Green eyes blinked.

"But Leah, I didn't push you I just tapped you in an angry way. You're being annoying."
Another slap.
This time, from Jack. AT 13, he was slowly slipping into substances, desperate to escape the chaos of the last few years. His parents got divorced. His mom was gay. He was being bullied at school. His best friend was a stoner, and his dad was an alcoholic who made empty promises. He hated his mom and resented Svetlana. No place felt safe.
Jack, you put a knife up towards me.
*You deserved it, Bi**h.*
He was only 13.
Slap across the face.
Flex. Hold. Breathe.

L eah's fingers hovered over her laptop keyboard, her heart pounding with a mix of excitement and trepidation. The sleek, modern office space provided by Club MIILFF buzzed with activity around her, a hive of ambitious women all working towards their dreams. The energy was palpable, electric, and Leah felt both energized and overwhelmed by it.

She took a deep breath, inhaling the scent of fresh coffee and new possibilities. The aroma of success, she thought wryly, wondering if Natasha could bottle and sell it as a MIILFF-branded perfume.

"You've got this, Leah," she whispered to herself, her mouse cursor hovering over the 'upload' button for her first "Corporate Minute" video.

The concept had come to her in a flash of inspiration during a late-night brainstorming session with Rava. They had been lounging in their cozy apartment, the New York City skyline twinkling beyond their windows like a constellation of urban stars.

"What if," Leah had mused, twirling a strand of her wild blonde hair, her eyes bright with the spark of an idea, "I could distill everything I've learned about climbing the corporate ladder into bite-sized, actionable tips?"

Rava, sprawled on their couch with a medical journal, had looked up with a grin that made Leah's heart skip a beat. Even after all this time, Rava's smile still had that effect on her. "You mean like a corporate fortune cookie, but actually useful?"

"Exactly!" Leah had exclaimed, her excitement bubbling over. She'd leapt up from her seat, pacing the room as the idea took shape. "Quick, punchy videos. One minute, one tip." She snapped her fingers, the sound sharp in the quiet apartment. "We'll call it 'The Corporate Minute.' Just a story, a funny skit, a real-life scenario, you know?"

Rava had set aside her journal, fully engaged now. "I love it. It's perfect for today's short attention spans. And who better give this advice than you? You've lived it, Leah. You've climbed that ladder. In Gucci sneakers!"

Now, sitting in her Club MIILFF office, Leah felt a flutter of nerves as she watched the upload progress bar inch toward completion. What if no one watched? What if they hated it? What if…?

"Leah!" A voice cut through her spiraling thoughts. "You're going to wear a hole in that desk with your tapping. Not even Herman Miller himself can save that desk from your knuckles."

She looked up to see Krystal, her leopard-print leggings somehow looking professional in the office setting. Beside her stood Reese, a whip-smart marketing guru assigned to Leah's business project by Club MIILFF's seemingly endless supply of connections, consultants, experts, tech geniuses, PR staff, and agents. Reese's dark curls bounced as she strode across the room, tablet in hand, her energy infectious.

"Sorry," Leah said, forcing her hands to still. "I'm just…"

"Nervous? Excited? Ready to conquer the world?" Reese finished for her, perching on the edge of Leah's swanky desk. Her smile was wide and confident, the kind of smile that made you believe anything was possible. "All of the above, I hope. Because girlllllll," she drawled the extra L's slowly, her eyes sparkling with enthusiasm, "we are about to set the internet on fire. No cap."

Leah couldn't help but smile at Reese's enthusiasm, even as she made a mental note to look up what "no cap" meant later. She was still getting used to the lingo of the younger generation. "You really think people will watch?"

Reese's perfectly arched eyebrow rose, her expression a mix of amusement and determination. "Watch? Leah, they're going to devour these videos like they're the last normal Jewish lesbian left in New York City." She inhaled as if it was her last breath, her passion for the project evident in every word. "Now, let's talk strategy."

Over the next few hours, Leah found herself swept up in a whirl-wind of marketing jargon she didn't fully understand. Social media, it seemed, required comprehension of phrases that sounded more like a foreign language than business terms. She nodded along as Reese and her team tossed around words like "algorithm optimiza-tion," "content curation," and "engagement metrics."

The Club MIILFF team moved with precision and energy, which left Leah both impressed and slightly dazed. Every few minutes, she heard a repetition of terms that were quickly becoming familiar.

"The algorithm!"

"Yep, it's the algorithm."

"Curated content."

"Ah yeah, content creation plan and agenda."

"Hashtags."

"Campaign."

"She definitely has the appeal. It's a MIILFF's time, you know? Women in their 40s are the new IT girls."

As the sun began to set, casting a warm glow through the floor-to-ceiling windows, Leah's phone buzzed. A text from Rava lit up the screen: "How's my corporate love doing? Watch the Olympics with me at home later?"

Leah smiled, her heart physically warming at the thought of curling up on the couch with Rava, leaving the whirlwind of the office behind. She quickly typed back: "Ugh. I wish. Things are crazy here. I'll fill you in later. The internet is a scary place, love..."

No sooner had she hit send, Reese's chirpy voice rang out again. "Leah! Your first video just hit 10,000 views!"

The office erupted in cheers, the sound of applause and excited chatter filling the space. Leah stared at Reese, stunned. "10k? And 2k shares?" She blinked, trying to process the information. "How is that even possible?"

Reese grinned, tapping her nose conspiratorially. Her eyes danced with a mixture of pride and mischief. "That, my dear, is the magic of a kick-ass marketing team and some very strategic influencer partnerships. But mostly," she added, her tone softening, "it's because you're damn good at what you do."

The next few weeks passed in a blur of filming, editing, and strategizing. Leah's "Corporate Minute" videos gained traction at a dizzying pace. Her inbox overflowed with messages from women thanking her for her advice, sharing their own stories of corporate triumphs and struggles. Each message touched her heart, reinforcing her belief in the importance of what she was doing.

"I hated my job, and after watching your videos, I realized I am the problem. Thank you for making me self-aware."

"Because of you, I learned how to ask for a raise. And now I even got a promotion!"

"You are so authentic and on point! As someone with ADHD, thank you for keeping your videos under 60 seconds!"

One evening, as Leah was packing up to head home at a reasonable hour, Ivanka finally popped into her office. The younger woman leaned against the doorframe, her posture casual but her eyes sharp and observant.

"You are working late too?" Ivanka asked, though it sounded more like a statement than a question. Leah smiled sheepishly, gesturing at the pile of papers on her desk. "Work never sleeps."

Ivanka's lips curved into a knowing smile. "Okay, but humans do. Come on, Leah, you can afford to go home and enjoy time with your girlfriend. Go!"

As if on cue, Leah's phone rang. The caller ID displayed an unfamiliar number with a New York area code. She glanced at Ivanka, who nodded encouragingly.

"Hello?" Leah answered, wedging the phone between her ear and shoulder as she continued to gather her things.

"Is this Leah Hart?" a crisp, professional voice inquired.

"Yes, this is she."

"Ms. Hart, this is Evelyn Marsh from HarperCollins Publishers. We've been following your 'Corporate Minute' series with great interest, and we'd like to discuss the possibility of a book deal."

Leah froze, her backpack slipping from her grasp and hitting the floor with a soft thud. She blinked rapidly, certain she must have misheard. "I'm sorry. Um," she took a deep breath, her free hand fluttering to her chest as she mouthed to Ivanka: 'OMG!'

Ivanka's eyes widened, and she moved closer, her interest piqued.

Leah put her mouth next to the phone again, struggling to keep her voice steady. "Um, did you say book deal?"

Evelyn chuckled, the sound warm and reassuring. "Yes, Ms. Hart. We believe your insights would translate beautifully to print. The audiences are very engaged; you've even been re-posted by Brene Brown and Simon Sinek."

Leah breathed heavily again, muting the call between breaths as she and Ivanka silently freaked out, their excitement manifesting in exaggerated gestures and silent screams.

"We're prepared to offer you a significant advance and a comprehensive marketing package, including a nationwide book tour," Evelyn continued, oblivious to the silent celebration happening on the other end of the line.

The world seemed to tilt on its axis. Leah gripped the edge of her desk, steadying herself. "I... wow. That's incredible. Can I have some time to think about it?"

"Of course," Evelyn replied, her tone understanding. "Take the weekend to consider. While we're on the call, I should also tell you that we're also considering turning the book into a movie. Think 'The Devil Wears Prada' meets 'The Office,' with you as the last of the millennial bosses! We haven't fleshed that out yet."

Leah was too stunned to respond, her mind reeling with possibilities.

"I'll email you the details of our offer, Leah. Is it LEEEEAH or LEAH?" Without waiting for a response, Evelyn continued, "We look forward to hearing from you."

As soon as the call ended, Leah sank into her chair, her mind reeling. A book deal. A tour. A potential movie. It was more than she'd ever dreamed possible when she'd started this journey. She looked up at Ivanka, who was beaming with pride and excitement.

They began to shriek at the same time, their professional composure forgotten in the face of such monumental news.

"Oh my gosh, I don't even know where to begin!" Leah exclaimed, her hands shaking as she ran them through her hair.

Ivanka laughed, her eyes sparkling. "That's where I come in, darling! Don't worry about a thing, Leah. I'll draft up contracts this weekend and ensure that we really are getting you the best deals and partnerships possible."

Leah smiled gratefully, feeling a wave of relief wash over her. "Really? Thank you, Ivanka. I know nothing about these stipulations and fine print. What a headache."

Ivanka patted Leah's hand reassuringly. "We will handle all the agreements. Leave that to us." She winked and left Leah's office, her heels clicking purposefully on the hardwood floor.

Alone again, Leah dialed Rava's number with shaking fingers.

"Hey, babe," Rava's warm voice answered. "Finally coming home?"

"Rava," Leah breathed, her voice filled with barely contained excitement, "you're not going to believe what just happened."

An hour later, Leah and Rava sat across from each other at their favorite corner table in Hummus Kitchen, a lowkey NYC local spot. A bottle of still water chilled beside them, neither one of them big drinkers.

"To my brilliant, beautiful, soon-to-be bestselling author," Rava toasted, raising her glass. Her eyes shone with pride and love, making Leah's heart swell.

Leah clinked her glass against Rava's, her cheeks flushed with excitement. "I still can't believe this is happening. Six weeks ago, I was just another corporate cog. Now..."

"Now you're changing lives," Rava finished for her, reaching across the table to squeeze Leah's hand. Her touch was warm and grounding. "I always knew you had it in you."

As they savored their laffas and tehina, Leah's phone buzzed incessantly with notifications. Another video is going viral, more followers, and more messages of thanks and support. The constant pings were a tangible reminder of how much her life had changed in such a short time.

"You know," Leah mused, setting down her pickle, her mind already racing with new ideas, "I think I need to expand the team. The demand is overwhelming."

Rava nodded, a thoughtful expression on her face. "What about creating a sales team? You could offer more personalized coaching services, maybe even corporate workshops."

Leah's eyes lit up, the idea taking root and blossoming in her mind. "Rava, you're a genius!"

"Duh, You bet I am." Rava laughed.

Leah smiled. "Yes, you are love!" She took a moment. "I could train a team to deliver the 'Corporate Minute' philosophy in person. We could reach so many more women that way." She paused, her expression softening as she gazed at her partner. "Ugh, you're so smart. And hot."

Rava giggled, deep red escaping her blushed face. She wasn't accustomed to compliments; her own childhood had been full of critique. But with Leah, she was learning to accept and even enjoy praise.

Their bubble was a safe one, a space where they could be fully themselves, supporting each other's dreams and ambitions. As they finished their meal, Leah felt a surge of gratitude for Rave's unwavering support and brilliant insights. She closed her eyes, remembering their first kiss.

Chapter Ten
Corporate Kiss

Kiss me....
I want you to kiss me ....

Leah's fingers trembled slightly as she pushed open the ornate doors of Royal Ancient Bathing, a high-end spa that had been all over her Instagram feed lately. The air inside was thick with the scent of eucalyptus and something else... was that lavender? She glanced at Rava, hoping to gauge her reaction.

Breathe. Stretch.

Rava's eyes were wide, taking in the opulent decor - all marble and gold leaf, with strategically placed Grecian urns that probably cost more than Leah's monthly rent. "Wow," Rava breathed, "this is... something."

Leah felt a flutter of pride. Third date, and she was already pulling out all the stops. Maybe this time, she'd have the courage to...

Her thoughts were interrupted as a staff member approached, all flowing robes and serene smile. "Welcome to Royal Ancient Bathing. I'm Starlight, and I'll be your guide today."

"Starlight?" Rava echoed, one eyebrow raised. "Is that your real name?"

The staff member's smile didn't waver. "It is for the next eight hours."

Leah stifled a giggle. She was starting to really like Rava's no-nonsense attitude. It was refreshing after years in the corporate world where everyone seemed to communicate entirely in buzzwords and fake smiles.

As Starlight led them towards the changing rooms, Rava suddenly stopped. "Wait," she said, her tone serious. "Before we go any further, I have some questions about your sanitation procedures."

Leah blinked in surprise. This was new.

What followed was a solid fifteen minutes of Rava grilling poor Starlight on everything from water filtration systems to towel washing temperatures. Leah watched, fascinated, as Rava pulled out a small notebook and started jotting down notes.

"And how often do you change the water in the communal pools?" Rava asked, her pen poised. Starlight's serene facade was starting to crack. "Um, I'm not sure of the exact schedule..."

"You're not sure?" Rava's voice rose an octave. "Do you realize the potential for bacterial growth in stagnant water? And in this humid environment? It's a veritable petri dish!"

Leah gently placed a hand on Rava's arm. "Hey," she said softly, "maybe we could save some questions for later? I'm sure everything is fine."

Rava took a deep breath, visibly calming herself. "You're right. I'm sorry. It's just... germs, you know?"

And suddenly, it clicked for Leah. The constant hand sanitizing, the way Rava always used a napkin to open doors, the slight hesitation before holding hands on their last date. Rava had OCD.

Instead of feeling put off, Leah felt a wave of affection wash over her. Rava wasn't perfect. She had her own struggles, her own quirks, just like Leah did.

As they changed into plush robes and made their way to the first bath, Leah found herself stealing glances at Rava. The way her brow furrowed slightly as she eyed the water, the determined set of her jaw as she finally lowered herself in. God, she was beautiful.

Leah wanted to kiss her so badly. Rava had tried on both of their previous dates, but Leah hadn't reciprocated. She was terrified of rejection, terrified of someone seeing her true self. She struggled to believe she was lovable as is and was sure Rava would leave her when she knew Leah's flaws.

They moved from bath to bath, the tension building between them. In the steam room, surrounded by the earthy scent of cedar, Rava turned to Leah, her eyes soft in the dim light.

"Leah," she said, her voice barely above a whisper, "I really like you."

Leah's heart pounded. This was it. Rava was leaning in, her lips parted slightly, and...

Panic seized Leah's chest. She couldn't breathe. Tears sprang to her eyes as she gasped for air, her body shaking. Yep, She was having an actual panic attack.

Instead of looking annoyed or put off, Rava just stood close to Leah. There was only concern in her eyes. And then, unexpectedly, a glimmer of humor. "You know," she said, her lips quirking into a smile, "most people wait until after the kiss to have this reaction."

Despite herself, Leah let out a watery chuckle.

Rava's smile widened. "There we go. That's better." She reached out, gently wiping a tear from Leah's cheek. "Now, Ms. Panic Attack, may I kiss you? I promise I brushed my teeth and gargled with antiseptic mouthwash beforehand."

Leah laughed again, the panic subsiding. She nodded, not trusting her voice.

And then Rava's lips were on hers, soft and warm and perfect. It was magic, better than any kiss Leah had ever experienced. When they finally pulled apart, both slightly breathless, Leah felt like she was floating.

"Wow," Rava murmured, her eyes sparkling. "You kiss like a guy."

Leah's eyes widened in horror. "Oh god, I'm so sorry, I."

But Rava was grinning. "No, I like it. A lot, actually."

Relief flooded through Leah, followed quickly by a wave of affection so strong it almost knocked her over. Here was this amazing woman who not only accepted Leah's panic attack and kissed her anyway but liked the way she kissed.

As they sat there in the steamy room, hands intertwined, Leah realized something. Maybe, just maybe, she was lovable exactly as she was. Panic attacks, guy-like kisses, and all.

"So," Rava said, breaking the comfortable silence, "want to go interrogate Starlight about their locker room sanitation next?"

Leah laughed, squeezing Rava's hand. "Only if you promise to kiss me again afterward." Rava's smile was brighter than all the gilded decorations in the spa combined. "Deal."

Chapter Eleven
Korporate Klimb

Who am I without my work ethic?
Who am I without achievement?
Without business?
I can sense. I'm more.
More than just being a Mrs.
Or a Mother.
What do I even like?
Who do I even like?
Why didn't I take the time to figure it out?
OH!!! Right. I had no other choice.
Until I made hard choices.
Mountain Pose

Ravas encouragement fueled excitement and newfound confidence in Leah. The next morning, Leah strode into the Club MIILFF offices with a new fire in her eyes. The click of her heels on the polished floor seemed to echo her determination.

"Reese!" she called out, spotting the marketing guru by the coffee machine. "We need to talk about expansion."

Reese looked up from her computer, a knowing smile playing on her lips. "I was wondering when you'd be ready for phase two." She lifted her glasses and adjusted her collar, her posture straightening as if preparing for battle. "Let's do this."

Over the next few months, Leah's brand exploded. She hired a team of sharp, ambitious women to act as her sales force, delivering workshops and coaching sessions across the country. Each woman brought her own unique perspective and experiences to the table, enriching the 'Corporate Minute' philosophy and expanding its reach.

Her book, "The Corporate Minute: 60 Seconds to Success," shot to the top of the New York Times bestseller list within weeks of its release. The cover, featuring Leah in a power suit with a stopwatch, became a familiar sight in bookstore windows and on subway ads across the city.

Mel, true to her word, was already working on turning the book into a screenplay. Her writer's block was a thing of the past as she poured her creativity into adapting Leah's story for the big screen.

"Look at you," Mel marveled one day as they met for coffee to discuss the script. Her eyes were wide with admiration and a hint of awe.

Leah smiled, reaching out to squeeze Mel's hand. "No, look at us!"

As Leah prepared for her nationwide book tour, she couldn't help but reflect on the whirlwind journey that had brought her here. From a young girl charging quarters for summer activities to a corporate climber, and now to this – a bona fide business mogul. The path hadn't been easy, but every struggle, every setback, had led her to this moment.

The night before her tour kicked off, Leah stood in front of her closet, agonizing over what to pack. Rava leaned against the doorframe, watching with amusement.

"You know," Rava said softly, her voice filled with emotion, "I am so incredibly proud of you."

Leah turned, a silk blouse dangling forgotten from her hand. She took in the sight of Rava, her partner, her rock, her biggest cheerleader. "I couldn't have done any of this without you. Your support, your ideas..."

Rava crossed the room, pulling Leah into a tight embrace. The familiar scent of her earthy smell enveloped Leah, comforting and exciting all at once. "This is all you, babe. Your brain, your drive, your heart. You're going to take this world by storm."

As they stood there, wrapped in each other's arms, Leah felt a sense of peace settle over her. Whatever challenges lay ahead on this tour, whatever new heights her career might reach, she knew she had the strength to face it all.

Because she wasn't just Leah anymore, she was Leah of "The Corporate Minute," the woman who had turned her struggles into success, her experiences into empire. And she was just getting started.

"I love you," Leah murmured into Rava's hair. "Thank you for believing in me, even when I didn't believe in myself."

Rava pulled back slightly, cupping Leah's face in her hands. "Always," she said simply before leaning in for a kiss that conveyed all the words left unsaid.

The next morning, as Leah prepared to leave for the airport, she found a small package on the kitchen counter. A note in Rava's handwriting was attached.

"For when you need a reminder of home. Go conquer the world, my love. - R"

Inside, Leah found a delicate silver locket. When she opened it, she saw a tiny picture of herself and Rava, laughing together in the sand, at one of Rava's favorite New Jersey beaches. On the other side was an inscription: "Every minute counts."

Blinking back tears, Leah fastened the locket around her neck. She took a deep breath, squared her shoulders, and headed out to face the world.

The book tour was a whirlwind of cities, faces, and stories. In every bookstore, conference hall, and TV studio, Leah shared her message of empowerment and efficiency. She met women from all walks of life, each with their own dreams and struggles.

In Chicago, a young intern asked how to make her voice heard in a male-dominated office. In Los Angeles, a senior executive sought advice on balancing career and family. In Houston, a group of women entrepreneurs hung on Leah's every word as she discussed negotiation tactics.

Through it all, Leah's phone buzzed constantly with updates from the Club MIILFF team. Reese's daily reports were a mix of impressive statistics and enthusiastic emojis.

"Video views up 200% this week!"

"3 Fortune 500 companies requesting workshops!"

"Mel says the screenplay's first draft is done!"

But it was the messages from Rava that Leah looked forward to most. Every night, no matter how late her events ran, she'd find a text waiting for her.

"Knocked 'em dead today, I bet. Miss you. Love you."

"Saw you on Good Morning America. You were brilliant. And hot."

"The apartment feels empty without you. But I'm so proud of where you are."

As the tour entered its final week, Leah found herself in Seattle, preparing for a keynote speech at a women's leadership conference. As she reviewed her notes in the green room, her phone rang. It was Ivanka.

"Leah, darling," Ivanka's voice was filled with barely contained excitement. "Are you sitting down?"

Leah laughed. "Yes, why? What's happened now?"

"We just got an offer from TED. They want you to do a TED Talk. The main stage, Leah. This is huge!"

Leah's mind reeled. A TED Talk? It was an opportunity beyond her wildest dreams. "Oh my god, Ivanka. That's... that's incredible!"

"It gets better," Ivanka continued. "Forbes wants to feature you in their '40 Under 40' list. And there's talk of a potential docuseries about female entrepreneurs, with you as the central focus."

As Ivanka rattled off more opportunities and accolades, Leah felt a strange mix of elation and overwhelm. This was everything she'd ever wanted, wasn't it? Success, recognition, and the chance to make a real difference in women's lives. So why did she suddenly feel so... lost?

"Leah? Are you still there?" Ivanka's voice cut through her thoughts.

"Yes, sorry," Leah said quickly. "This is all wonderful news. I just... I need some time to process it all. Can we discuss details when I'm back in New York?"

After ending the call, Leah sat in silence for a long moment. Then, almost without thinking, she dialed Rava's number.

"Hey, superstar," Rava answered on the second ring. "Isn't it almost time for your speech?"

"Yeah, it is," Leah said, her voice small. "Rava, I... I think I'm having a panic attack."

"Oh, love," Rava's voice softened with concern. "What's going on?"

The words tumbled out of Leah in a rush. She told Rava about the TED Talk, the Forbes list, and the docuseries. About how her life had become a non-stop whirlwind of opportunities and obligations. About how she was terrified of letting everyone down, of not living up to the image of success she'd created.

"And the worst part," Leah finished, her voice cracking, "is that I miss you. I miss our life. I miss who I was before all of this."

There was a moment of silence on the other end of the line. Then Rava spoke, her voice filled with love and understanding.

"Leah, listen to me. You are still you. The same brilliant, compassionate, slightly neurotic woman I fell in love with. All of this success? It's because people see in you what I've always seen. But if it's not making you happy, if it's too much, you have the power to change it."

Leah took a shaky breath. "But how? I can't just walk away from all of this."

"No, but you can set boundaries. You can say no to things that don't align with your values or your happiness. Remember what you always say in your videos? 'Your time is your most valuable asset. Invest it wisely.'"

Leah couldn't help but laugh. "Using my own advice against me? That's low, Rava."

"Hey, if the minutiae fit," Rava teased before her tone turned serious again. "You've got this, Leah. Go give that speech. Inspire those women. And when you come home, we'll figure out the rest together. Okay?"

"Okay," Leah said, feeling the panic recede. "I love you, you know that?"

"I love you too. Now, go be amazing."

Leah laughed, "No, you Dr. Ris. You go to be amazing."

As Leah ended the call, she caught sight of herself in the mirror. She touched the locket around her neck, took a deep breath, and smiled. She was Leah Hart, creator of The Corporate Minute. But more than that, she was a woman who had fought for her dreams, who had built a life and a love she was proud of.

With renewed purpose, she gathered her notes and headed for the stage. It was time to share her minute – and her truth – with the world.

As she stepped into the spotlight, the applause washing over her, Leah felt a sense of clarity she hadn't experienced in months. She knew that whatever came next – whether it was a TED Talk or a quiet night at home with Rava – she had the strength to face it.

Because every minute counted, and she was determined to make each one matter.

Chapter Twelve
Business Battles

He loves me
He gives me all his money
Never mind what I had to do to get these diamonds
Never again
I'm way too good for this necklace
I'm conceited, undefeated
I don't need to be humble
I ulreudy know how great I am.

M el stared at the blinking cursor on her laptop screen, its rhythmic pulsing a mocking reminder of the words she couldn't seem to find. The screenplay adaptation of Leah's "The Corporate Minute" book lay half-finished, a digital testament to her writer's block.

She sighed, pushing away from her desk and moving to the window of her small Brooklyn apartment. The city sprawled before her, a tapestry of lights and shadows, each pinprick of brightness representing a story she longed to tell.

"Come on, Mel," she muttered to herself, "you used to be good at this."

The truth was, Mel hadn't felt like a real writer in months. The writers' strike had initially seemed like a blessing in disguise – a chance to focus on her personal projects, to rediscover her voice. Instead, it had become a void, a gaping chasm of time that she struggled to fill with meaningful work.

And then there was Club MIILFF. Mel chuckled softly, remembering the skepticism she'd felt when Natasha first invited them. Who would have thought that a club with such a provocative name would become a lifeline?

She thought back to the day Leah had asked her to adapt "The Corporate Minute" for the screen. The excitement in Leah's eyes, the faith she had in Mel's abilities – it had been intoxicating. For the first time in ages, Mel had felt like a real writer again.

But now, as the deadline loomed and the words refused to come, doubt crept in like a poison. Was she really cut out for this? Had she been fooling herself – and everyone else – all along?

Mel's phone buzzed, startling her from her reverie. A text from Maddie: "Hey girl, you coming to the MIILFF mixer tonight? Lots of bigwigs from the industry gonna be there. Could be good for your career!"

Mel hesitated, her thumb hovering over the reply button. The thought of networking, of putting on a brave face and pretending everything was fine, made her stomach churn. But then again, wasn't that what being a professional was all about?

She typed out a quick "Sure, see you there!" before she could change her mind.

As she rummaged through her closet for something suitable to wear, Mel's mind wandered to the ethical dilemma that had been nagging at her for weeks. The screenplay was coming along well (writer's block notwithstanding), but there was a part of Leah's story that Mel had been struggling with – the part about leveraging connections and influence to fast-track success.

On one hand, it was a reality of the business world. Networking, using your contacts, seizing opportunities – these were all part of climbing the corporate ladder. But on the other hand, didn't it perpetuate a system of privilege and inequality? How could she write about it without either condoning it or condemning it?

Mel slipped on a sleek black dress, the fabric cool against her skin. She caught sight of herself in the mirror and paused. Who was this woman staring back at her? A successful screenwriter on the verge of her big break? Or an imposter, playing dress-up in a world she didn't truly belong in?

She thought about her journey – a queer polyamorous masculine-centered woman navigating the predominantly white, male world of Hollywood. The challenges she'd faced, the doors that had been closed in her face. And now, thanks to Club MIILFF, those same doors were swinging open.

But at what cost? Was she compromising her values for success? Or was she simply playing the game, using the tools at her disposal to level a playing field that had been tilted against her from the start?

As she applied her lipstick, a final touch of armor for the evening ahead, Mel made a decision. She would go to the mixer, yes. She would network and schmooze and do all the things expected of an up-and-coming screenwriter. But she would also be honest – with herself and with others.

She would write Leah's story, but she would write it her way. She would show the complexities and gray areas. She would celebrate the triumphs but also acknowledge the cost. And maybe, just maybe, she could create something that was both true to Leah's experience and true to her own values.

Mel grabbed her keys and headed for the door, a new sense of purpose in her step. As she locked up, her neighbor, Mrs. Goldstein, poked her head out.

"Going somewhere fancy, Melissa?" the older woman asked, eyeing Mel's outfit appreciatively.

Mel smiled. "Just a work thing, Mrs. G. Wish me luck?"

Mrs. Goldstein's eyes twinkled. "Luck? Pah! You don't need luck. You've got talent, brains, and chutzpah. That's better than luck any day."

Mel felt a warmth spread through her chest. "Thanks, Mrs. G. I needed to hear that."

As she made her way down the stairs and out into the Brooklyn night, Mel felt the first stirrings of excitement. Yes, she had doubts. Yes, she was struggling. But she was also growing, learning, and evolving. She was becoming not just a better writer but a better person.

The city pulsed around her, full of stories waiting to be told. And Mel was ready to tell them – her way.

She pulled out her phone and fired off a quick text to Leah: "Hey, can we meet tomorrow? I've got some ideas for the screenplay I want to run by you."

As she slipped her phone back into her purse, Mel smiled to herself. The blank page wasn't an obstacle anymore. It was an opportunity. An opportunity to write her own story on her own terms.

And she couldn't wait to see how it would unfold.

CHAPTER THIRTEEN
WHAT IS FREEDOM

360
I went my own way, and I made it
I'm your favorite reference baby
Breathe. Just breathe.
AM I EVEN BEING HEARD!!!!!
I really am sick of being codependent.
Why do I feel the need to absorb my partner's energy? Why do I personalize
so much?
Maybe the reasons don't matter anymore, Leah.
But - I'm codependent.
But - That's just a label
Fine. I get it.
This self-love thing is hard.
Stretch. Breathe.
Bumping that…

Natasha sprawled across her plush velvet couch, kicking off her stilettos with a sigh of relief. The Manhattan skyline twinkled beyond her penthouse windows, a glittering reminder of all she'd achieved. And yet, as she massaged her aching feet, she couldn't shake the feeling that something was missing.

"Another day, another dollar," she muttered, reaching for the bottle of vodka on her coffee table. It was the good stuff, imported straight from Moscow – a little taste of the homeland she'd never known.

As the fiery liquid slid down her throat, Natasha's mind wandered to her parents. Mama and Papa Petrova, fresh off the boat from St. Petersburg, wide-eyed and hopeful in their new American home. They'd arrived with nothing but dreams and a battered suitcase full of memories.

"We come for better life, Natasha," her mother would say, her accent thick even after years in the States. "You have chances we never had."

Chances. Natasha almost laughed at the thought. What her parents hadn't realized was that in America, chances didn't come for free. You had to fight for them, claw your way up from the bottom, and never, ever stop hustling.

And hustle she had. From the moment she could walk, Natasha had been working angles. Selling lemonade on street corners, running errands for the neighborhood babushkas, even starting a lucrative playground business trading rare Pokémon cards.

School had never been her thing. While other kids buried their noses in books, Natasha was out there, learning the language of the streets, the art of the deal. By sixteen, she'd dropped out entirely, much to her parents' dismay.

"Education is key to success!" her father had bellowed, his face red with anger and disappointment.

But Natasha knew better. In her world, success wasn't about degrees or diplomas. It was about connections, about knowing how to read people, how to give them what they wanted – or what they didn't even know they wanted yet.

She'd bounced from job to job, scheme to scheme. Waitressing, bartending, promotions, even a brief stint as a hand model. Each gig was a steppingstone, a chance to meet people, to expand her network. And with every new connection, every hustled dollar, Natasha had clawed her way up the social ladder.

Then came Club MIILFF. At first, it seemed like just another angle to work. Rich, powerful women looking for a sense of community and empowerment? It was a gold mine waiting to be tapped.

Natasha took another swig of vodka, remembering the day she'd met Meryl and Ivanka. She'd turned on the charm, spinning tales of her imaginary business successes, dropping names she'd only read about in Forbes. And they'd bought it hook, line, and sinker.

Before she knew it, she was in. Not just in, but integral to the operation. Her knack for spotting potential, for reeling in new members, had made her indispensable. Each new MIILFF she brought in, each successful business she helped launch, meant a fat commission check in her pocket.

It was the ultimate hustle. And for a while, it had been enough.

But lately... lately, something had changed. They were asking her to minimize worry, gaslighting her into turning the other cheek when she was concerned about shady ongoings, and most recently, when she questioned Meryl on what happened to Naomi, they told her that Naomi had a mental breakdown and that day in the elevator when she yelled at Natasha, she had a manic episode.

Natasha stood, padding barefoot to the floor-to-ceiling windows. She pressed her forehead against the cool glass, staring out at the city she'd conquered.

"What's it all for?" she whispered, her breath fogging the window.

The truth was, Natasha was tired. Tired of the constant hustle, the never-ending grind. Tired of pretending to be someone she wasn't, of living up to an image she'd created but never truly inhabited.

She thought of the women she recruited for Club MIILFF. The real MIILFFs – mothers with careers, with families, with a purpose beyond the next big score. Women like Leah, balance ambition with love success with fulfillment.

For the first time in her life, Natasha felt a pang of envy. Not for their money or their status – she had plenty of both. No, what she envied was their sense of belonging, of authenticity. Their ability to be... well, real.

"Real," Natasha scoffed, turning away from the window. "What the hell does that even mean?"

But deep down, she knew. It meant having something – someone – to come home to. It meant creating something lasting, something that would outlive the next trend or the next big deal. It meant being more than just a pretty face or a skilled negotiator.

It meant being a mother.

The thought hit her like a punch to the gut. Natasha, the eternal hustler, the woman who prided herself on needing no one, wanting a child? It was absurd. And yet...

She thought of little Andrew, Maddie's son. The way his eyes lit up when he saw her, his chubby arms reaching out for a hug. "Auntie Tasha!" he'd squeal, and for a moment, just a moment, Natasha felt... whole.

"Bozhe moi," she muttered, reverting to her parents' native tongue. "What am I thinking?"

But the seed had been planted. As she poured another shot of vodka, Natasha's mind raced with possilities. Could she do it? Could she, Natasha Petrova, become a real MIILFF?

It would mean slowing down, settling down. It would mean being vulnerable, opening herself up to love and loss and all the messy parts of life she'd spent so long avoiding.

It would mean, in short, the biggest hustle of her life.

Natasha downed the shot, relishing the burn. Then, with a decisive nod, she reached for her phone. Her fingers flew over the keys as she typed out a message to Ivanka.

"Need to talk. Time for a new angle on the MIILFF thing. My place, tomorrow, 9 AM. Bring coffee."

As she hit send, Natasha felt a familiar thrill course through her veins. The thrill of a new challenge, a new mountain to climb. But this time, it wasn't about money or status or power.

This time, it was about becoming real. Becoming whole. Becoming, perhaps for the first time in her life, truly herself.

Natasha Petrova, the eternal hustler, was about to embark on her greatest adventure yet. And God help anyone who tried to stand in her way.

CHAPTER FOURTEEN
BUSINESS WITH BARRY BREATHE

I'm a good pretender
Would you come to see my show ...
I've got lots of problems
Good thing nobody knows ...

Mel paced the length of her small Brooklyn apartment, her short, spiky hair standing on end from running her fingers through it repeatedly. The golden afternoon light streaming through the windows did nothing to calm her frayed nerves. Her emerald eyes, usually sparkling with mischief, were clouded with worry as she stared at her phone, willing it to ring.

"Come on, come on," she muttered, glancing at the clock for the hundredth time. "It's been three days. How long does it take to read a damn screenplay?"

As if on cue, her phone burst into life, the ringtone echoing off the exposed brick walls. Mel's heart leaped into her throat. She fumbled with the device, nearly dropping it in her haste to answer.

"Hello?" she answered, her voice barely above a whisper.

"Mel, darling!" Barry Arthur Dunway's booming voice filled the line. "I've got fabulous news. The studio loves your screenplay! They want to fast-track it for next summer's blockbuster season."

Mel's knees went weak, and she sank onto her worn leather couch. "That's... that's incredible, Mr. Barry Arthur Dunway. I can't believe it."

She couldn't. This was her dream. And here it was. A reality.

"Please, call me Arthur. We're practically family now!" He chuckled. "Now, there are just a few tiny changes they want to make. Nothing major, I assure you. Just creative touches." He paused. "Why don't you come down to the office tomorrow, and we'll go over everything?"

"Of course, of course," Mel agreed, her mind racing. "What time should I be there?" "Let's say 10 AM. That'll give us plenty of time to chat before lunch. Oh, and Mel?" "Yes?"

"Wear something nice. You never know who you might run into in these hallways. Could be your future leading lady!"

As Mel hung up, a mix of elation and trepidation swirled in her stomach. Her screenplay, Her Baby, was going to be a movie. A MOVIE!

But what changes did they want to make?

She dialed Leah's number, needing to share the news with someone who'd understand. "Leah? You're not going to believe this..."

The next morning, Mel stood outside the imposing glass and steel structure that housed Dunway Productions. She smoothed down her blazer, a vintage find that she hoped struck the right balance between professional, sexy, and creative.

"You've got this, Mel," she whispered to herself. "It's your story. Your vision."

As she stepped into the lobby, the hustle and bustle of Hollywood hit her full force. Assistants scurried about with coffee orders, actors practiced lines in corners, and the constant buzz of phones created a cacophony of importance.

Mel approached the reception desk, where a bored-looking young man was scrolling through his phone.

"Excuse me," Mel said, clearing her throat. "I'm here to see Arthur Dunway."

The receptionist looked up, his eyes widening slightly as he took in Mel's appearance. "Oh, you must be the new writer everyone's talking about. Mel, right?"

Mel blinked, surprised. "Everyone's talking about me?"

He nodded, a conspiratorial grin spreading across his face. "Honey, when Arthur Dunway fast tracks a project, everyone notices. You're the talk of the town."

Before Mel could process this information, a whirlwind in Louboutins appeared at her side.

"You must be Mel! I'm Cynthia, Arthur's personal assistant. He's so excited to meet with you. Come on, I'll take you up."

As they rode the elevator, Cynthia chatted away, filling Mel in on office gossip she neither knew nor cared about. But one tidbit caught her attention.

"...and of course, everyone's wondering who they'll cast as Zoe. I heard Scarlett Johansson's team reached out, but personally, I think Zendaya would be perfect."

Mel's head spun. Scarlett Johansson? Zendaya? These were A-list stars, and they were considering her characters.

The elevator doors opened to reveal a plush corridor lined with movie posters. Cynthia led Mel to a set of imposing oak doors.

"Here we are! Good luck in there, sweetie. And if you need anything at all, just give me a shout."

Mel took a deep breath and pushed open the doors. Arthur Dunway's office was exactly as she'd imagined – opulent, filled with awards and memorabilia, and with a view of the Hollywood sign perfectly framed in the floor-to-ceiling windows.

Arthur, a silver-haired fox with a megawatt smile, rose from behind his massive desk to greet her.

"Mel, my dear! So wonderful to finally meet you in person. Please, have a seat."

As Mel settled into a plush leather chair, three different assistants popped in in rapid succession, offering tea, coffee, and a selection from Uber Eats.

"No, really," the last one said, batting her eyelashes at Mel. "Whatever you need, I am so here."

"*So here,*" Mel thought. "*Was she even 20?*"

Arthur shooed the assistants away with a wave of his hand. "Now, Mel. Let's talk about your screenplay. It's brilliant, truly. You've got raw talent, my dear."

Mel smiled, a warm glow of pride spreading through her chest. "Thank you, Mr. D."

"Arthur, please," he interrupted with a wink.

"Arthur," Mel corrected herself. "I put my heart into this screenplay. It's a story I've been wanting to tell for as long as I could write."

Arthur nodded, his expression softening. "And it shows, believe me. The depth of emotion, the complexity of the relationships... it's all there." He paused, leaning forward. "But..."

Mel's heart sank. There it was. The dreaded 'but'.

"We need to make it pop," Arthur continued. "Give it that summer blockbuster sizzle, you know?"

Mel nodded uncertainly, not sure where Arthur was going with this.

"I'm thinking," he paused dramatically, "a few subtle changes."

"Subtle?" Mel echoed, her voice barely above a whisper.

Arthur whipped out a list from a binder on his oak desk. "Yes, tasteful. For example, I took some notes with my suggestions."

As Arthur outlined the changes, Mel's heart sank further with each word. Gone was the nuanced exploration of female friendship, the story she had held onto for almost 40 years of her life. In its place, a formulaic, sensationalized romance and contrived action sequences with typical typecast female roles. Her strong, complex protagonist had been reduced to a damsel in distress.

"But... that's not the story I wrote," Mel protested weakly.

Arthur waved his hand dismissively. "Trust me, Mel. This is what sells. You're inexperienced. This is what we do in Hollywood." He leaned in, his voice dropping to a conspiratorial whisper. "And think of the paycheck, darling. You'll never have to worry about rent again. In fact, there's a good chance that you can probably buy the apartment with the advance alone."

He scribbled on his notepad and waved the numbers in Mel's direction. The figure was astronomical. She could buy two Brooklyn apartments for that amount.

But her story was gone.

"I... I need some time to think about this," Mel managed to say, her mouth dry.

Arthur's smile never faltered. "Of course, of course. Take the weekend. But remember, Mel, opportunities like this don't come along every day. We need to strike while the iron is hot."

Mel left the office in a daze, her mind a battlefield of conflicting emotions. The promise of financial security warred with her artistic integrity. As she wandered the bustling New York streets, she found herself outside the CLUB MIILFF building.

Almost on autopilot, she entered and made her way to the I DO headquarters. The familiar scent of Chanel welcomed her, along with Mimi's radiant smile.

"Mel! What a lovely surprise," Mimi exclaimed, rising gracefully from her yoga mat in the corner of her office. Her lithe form moved with fluid grace as she approached Mel.

Mel's breath caught in her throat. Mimi's presence always had this effect on her, a mixture of admiration and something... more.

"Mimi, I... I need advice," Mel stammered, sinking into a plush chair.

As Mel poured out her dilemma, Mimi listened intently, her dark eyes full of compassion. When Mel finished, Mimi took her hands gently.

"Mel, you have a gift. Your words, your vision... they matter. Don't let anyone dim your light for the sake of a paycheck."

Mel felt a warmth spread through her at Mimi's touch and words. "But the money... it could change everything for me."

Mimi smiled knowingly. "Money without fulfillment is an empty victory. Trust me, I've been there. Remember why you started writing in the first place."

As they talked, Mel found herself opening up about more than just her screenplay. She shared her dreams, her fears, and, without meaning to, she instinctively leaned in to kiss Mimi.

Mimi's eyes widened in surprise, then softened with affection. "Oh, Mel," she said gently, "I'm flattered, truly. But you know I'm not..."

"Polyamorous," Mel finished for her, a sad smile on her face. "I know. I just... I couldn't help myself."

Mimi squeezed Mel's hand. "Your heart has so much love to give. The right person – or people – will cherish that about you. But those aren't my choices." Her voice lowered. " I want one person."

Mel was mortified. Seeing this, Mimi immediately softened. She let out a small breath and swiftly changed the subject.

"Now, let's focus on your screenplay. That's a love story worth fighting for."

Mel spent the next two hours ironing out her approach, with Mimi as her sounding board.

"You've got this," Mimi said, pulling Mel into a warm, encouraging hug.

As Mel left CLUB MIILFF that evening, her head was clearer than it had been in days. She knew what she had to do.

The next morning, bright and early, she marched into Arthur Dunway's office, green eyes blazing with determination.

"Do you have an appointment–" the receptionist began, blinking in surprise. "No. I don't," Mel responded as she walked right into Arthur's large office.

Arthur looked up from his desk, his eyebrows rising in surprise. "Mel! I wasn't expecting you until…"

"Arthur," she announced, cutting him off, "I can't accept these changes. My story matters, and I won't compromise its integrity."

Arthur's eyes sparkled, and Mel felt a momentary flash of terror. Had she just thrown away her one shot at the big time?

Arthur took a deep breath. "I like your fire. I want your screenplay."

Mel remained even keeled, though her heart was racing. "It's for sale. On my terms."

Arthur's eyebrows shot up even higher. "Even if you miss out on the opportunity of a lifetime?"

Mel stood her ground. "Is it the opportunity of a lifetime if you rob me of my story? I'm choosing the opportunity to be true to myself and my art. There are other ways to achieve financial freedom without selling my soul."

Arthur laughed, a deep, genuine belly laugh that took Mel completely by surprise.

"I love it!" he exclaimed, still chuckling. "Okay, Mel. Your story, the way you like it. I'll tell Ivanka to draft up the contract."

Mel blinked, stunned. "Just like that?"

Arthur leaned back in his chair, a newfound respect in his eyes. "Just like that. You know, Mel, in this business, everyone's always saying yes to me. It's refreshing to meet someone with the guts to say no."

"But... what about all those changes you wanted?"

Arthur waved his hand dismissively. "Standard procedure. We always push to see how much we can get away with. But your story? It's gold as it is. That's why I wanted it in the first place."

Mel felt a wave of relief wash over her, followed quickly by a surge of pride. She'd stood her ground, and it had paid off.

"This really was some family business," Mel observed, thinking of Ivanka doing the contracts and Arthur's ex-wife referring writers.

She turned to say goodbye to Arthur, but he was already yelling at an agent on the phone. "Get me the kid actor. I don't give a damn what else he's doing right now. Bring me the kid."

As she walked out of the office, head held high, Mel felt a weight lift from her shoulders. She didn't just make a small fortune; she had reclaimed something far more valuable – her voice.

Her phone buzzed with a text from Mimi: "Yoga and smoothies later? You look like you could use some zen."

Mel smiled, her heart full. She might not have Mimi's love in the way she wanted, but she had her friendship and support. And right now, that felt like more than enough.

As she stepped onto the busy New York street, Mel felt like she was seeing the world with new eyes. The path ahead was uncertain, but for the first time in a long while, she was excited to see where it might lead. Her story was going to be told—her way.

She dialed Leah's number, bursting to share the news.

"Leah? You're not going to believe what just happened..."

As Mel recounted her showdown with Arthur, Leah's excited squeals echoed through the phone. "Mel, you badass!" Leah exclaimed. "We need to celebrate. MIILFF night out?" Mel grinned. "Absolutely. But first, I promised Mimi I'd meet her for yoga and smoothies."

"Ooh, MIMI!" Leah teased. "Any progress on that front?"

Mel sighed. "Not exactly. But you know what? I'm okay with that. She's an amazing friend, and right now, that's what I need most."

"Well, look at you, all grown up and mature," Leah laughed. "Alright, go get your zen on. But tonight, we paint the town red!"

As Mel made her way to meet Mimi, she couldn't help but reflect on how much her life had changed since joining CLUB MIILFF. She had found a community, rediscovered her passion, and now, she was on the brink of seeing her dream realized on the big screen.

The future was bright, and Mel was ready to embrace it, one scene at a time.

CHAPTER FIFTEEN
BUSINESS BABY

I had to escape
The city was sticky and cruel
It is
Isn't it
Breathe

The Club MIILFF conference room was abuzz with chatter as members filtered in for the monthly meeting. The air was thick with the scent of designer perfumes and freshly brewed coffee. Leah and Mel were huddled in a corner, their heads close together as they animatedly discussed their latest project.

"I'm telling you, Mel," Leah said, her eyes sparkling with excitement, "if we can pull this off, it'll be groundbreaking. A reality show that empowers women instead of pitting them against each other?"

Mel nodded enthusiastically, her curly hair bouncing with the movement. "I love it. But you know the network execs will push for more drama. We'll have to be strategic about how we pitch it."

Across the room, Maddie was perched on the edge of a sleek leather chair, her phone held out as she showed Krystal a series of photos. Little Andrew, with his mop of unruly brown curls and gap-toothed grin, beamed from the screen.

"Oh my god, he's gotten so big!" Krystal cooed, zooming in on a picture of Andrew in an adorable dinosaur backpack. "How was his first day?"

Maddie's face softened with maternal pride. "It was... emotional. For me, mostly. He just marched right in like he owned the place. Didn't even look back."

"That's our little MIILFF-in-training," Krystal laughed, patting Maddie's arm comfortingly.

Suddenly, the double doors burst open with a dramatic flourish, and in strode Natasha. Her signature leopard-print leggings were stretched tight over a noticeably rounded belly, paired with a flowing crimson blouse that did little to hide her new curves. Her fiery red hair was swept up in an elegant chignon, and her green eyes sparkled with mischief.

"Ladies," she announced, her voice cutting through the chatter like a hot knife through butter, "your favorite Russian doll is about to become a Matryoshka!"

The room fell silent for a beat before erupting into a cacophony of squeals, gasps, and exclamations. Chairs scraped against the floor as everyone rushed to surround Natasha.

"Oh my god, Natasha!" Leah was the first to reach her, enveloping her in a tight hug. She pulled back, her hands on Natasha's shoulders, eyes wide with disbelief. "You're pregnant? How? When? Who?"

Natasha smirked, her eyes twinkling with mischief. "Well, darling, when a woman attractive like me meets a man..."

"Natasha!" Maddie gasped, clapping her hands over Andrew's ears. The toddler, however, was far more interested in the chocolate chip cookie he was munching on than the 'adults' conversation. Crumbs tumbled down his shirt as he grinned up at the women, oblivious to the excitement.

"Oh, relax," Natasha laughed, waving a perfectly manicured hand dismissively. "I'm just joking! I've actually gone ahead and gotten a donor." She paused dramatically, savoring the anticipation on her friends' faces. "Yeah, some hot gay guy from Italy asked me for eggs, and we had a whole switcher legal deal." She nodded sagely. "They do that now."

The room fell into a stunned silence, everyone processing this unexpected information. Natasha, never one to let a moment go to waste, continued with a wink, "What? I have more eggs! Obviously. Bun in the oven."

Mel shook her head, a grin spreading across her face. "Only you, Natasha, could make a super-planned pregnancy sound like the setup for a joke."

Ivanka, who had been quietly observing from the corner, her sharp blue eyes taking in every detail, stepped forward. Her platinum blonde hair was pulled back in a severe bun, and her crisp white blazer practically screamed 'business.' "Well, this is certainly unexpected. But if anyone can turn an unexpected pregnancy into a business opportunity, it's you, Natasha." Her lips curved into a knowing smile. "So, spill. What's the angle?"

Natasha's grin widened, her green eyes sparkling with excitement. "I'm so glad you asked, darling. Ladies, prepare yourselves for the next big thing in MIILFF entertainment!" She paused for dramatic effect, one hand resting on her belly while the other gestured grandly. "I present to you: 'What to Expect When You Don't Have a Husband with a Baby on the Way' – a groundbreaking documentary series following yours truly through the wild world of single motherhood!"

The room erupted in laughter and applause. Krystal, her curvy figure squeezed into a hot pink dress, clapped her hands together in delight. "That's brilliant!" she exclaimed. "We could have episodes on everything from navigating dating while pregnant to building a nursery with zero handyman skills!"

"Ooh, and a special on pregnancy-safe cocktails!" chimed in Reese, already typing furiously on her tablet. Her glasses slid down her nose as she looked up, a mischievous glint in her eye. "We could call it 'Virgin on the Ridiculous'!"

Itta piped in. "I can do a whole eating for two series! Chef Itta approved Girl Grill items plus ones!"

As the women bounced ideas back and forth, each more outrageous than the last, Natasha basked in the glow of their excitement. For once, she wasn't hustling or putting on an act. This was real – terrifyingly, exhilaratingly real.

"So," Mel said, slinging an arm around Natasha's shoulders, her dark curls mingling with Natasha's fiery locks, "how does it feel to be a genuine MIILFF-in-training finally?"

Natasha placed a hand on her belly, a soft smile playing on her lips. The vulnerability in her expression was something her friends rarely saw. "Honestly? It feels like the biggest hustle of my life. But also... the most authentic." She looked around at the beaming faces of her friends, her voice thick with emotion. "I couldn't have done this without all of you. My little Vodka Junior is going to have the fiercest, most fabulous aunties in all of New York."

"Vodka Junior?" Leah raised an eyebrow, her tone a mix of amusement and concern. "Please tell me that's not going to be the baby's actual name."

"Of course not," Natasha scoffed, rolling her eyes dramatically. "I'm thinking something more traditional. Like Chanel. Or Gucci."

Mimi, who had been unusually quiet, suddenly piped up, her eyes shining with excitement. "I can definitely plan a fun baby shower!" She immediately transformed into what the group affectionately called her 'I DO Mode,' whipping out a small notebook and pen from her purse. "We could do a 'Bun in the Oven' theme, with little bread-shaped favors and…"

As laughter filled the room once more, Natasha felt a warmth spread through her chest that had nothing to do with pregnancy hormones. This was family. This was belonging. This was real.

"Alright, MIILFFs," she called out, clapping her hands together to bring focus back to the group. Her voice took on the commanding tone that had made her such a successful businesswoman. "Enough sentimentality. We've got a groundbreaking, boundary-pushing, possibly FCC-violating show to plan. Who's ready to make some motherhood magic?"

The resounding cheer that followed was answered enough. As the meeting dissolved into a flurry of ideas and planning, with Mimi scribbling furiously in her notebook and Reese creating an impromptu vision board on her tablet, Natasha couldn't help but think that maybe, just maybe, this whole "real MIILFF" thing wasn't going to be so bad after all.

Especially if she could turn it into a hit show along the way.

In the midst of the excitement, Leah found herself drifting back to a memory she'd rather forget. Her hands clenched involuntarily as she thought of another Andrew – her toxic former colleague. His smug face swam before her eyes, along with the memory of his inconsistent messages and infuriating behavior.

She remembered asking him once, in a moment of frustration, what she should do if she needed clearer communication. His response still made her blood boil: he had rolled his eyes and scoffed, "Leah, if you need more clarity, go find it."

The contrast between Andrew and the sweet little boy munching on cookies across the room couldn't have been starker. Leah took a deep breath, pushing the negative thoughts aside. She was tired of searching for kernels of clarity when others were emotionally immature word-salads.

"What a tuchis that Andrew was," she muttered under her breath. "Perfect example of Corporate BS wrapped in a polite bow with a side of more BS."

"Did you say something, Leah?" Mel asked, glancing at her friend with concern.

Leah shook her head, plastering on a smile. "Nothing important. Just thinking out loud." She turned her attention back to the group, determined to focus on the positivity and excitement of the moment. This was what mattered – her chosen family, supporting each other through life's adventures, no matter how unexpected they might be.

As the meeting continued, filled with laughter, outrageous ideas, and genuine warmth, Leah felt the last of her negative thoughts melt away. Whatever challenges lay ahead – for Natasha, for the group, for all of them individually – they would face them together, with humor, grace, and a healthy dose of MIILFF attitude.

CHAPTER SIXTEEN
MOTHER'S DAUGHTER

Don't mess with my Freedom
I came up to get me some
There must be something in the water
Or that I'm my mother's daughter ...Halleluja
Balance. Breathe
Are you ever going to acknowledge how much Jack hurt you?
I'm not sure. I don't even wanna voice it
Why?
Because that makes it real
OK, but it was real
It was, wasn't it?
What about your mother?
Will you ever allow yourself to grieve her death?
I don't deserve to grieve!!!
Yes You Do.

The rhythmic click-clack of Louboutin's echoed through the marbled halls of Club MIILFF headquarters, the sound amplified by the tension in the air. Leah's fingers tightened around her oat milk latte, the warmth seeping through the biodegradable cup a stark contrast to the chill running down her spine. As she rounded the corner, she nearly collided with a frantic-looking Mel.

"Whoa there, you are training for the New York Marathon or what?" Leah quipped, steadying her drink and taking in Mel's disheveled appearance. A wild, panicked look replaced the usual sparkle in Mel's emerald eyes.

Mel's pixie cut, typically a masterpiece of precision styling, looked like it had gone ten rounds with a tornado and lost. "Leah! Thank God. Have you seen Maddie? I can't get hold of her," she blurted out, words tumbling over each other in her haste.

Leah frowned, concern creeping into her voice like ivy on a neglected trellis. "No, I haven't. What's going on?"

Mel ran a hand through her hair, making it stand up even more. She looked like she'd stuck her finger in an electrical socket – if electrical sockets dispensed pure, unadulterated worry. "She was supposed to meet me for coffee this morning and just... didn't show up."

"Did you try texting?" Leah asked, pulling out her phone, its rose gold case glinting under the soft lighting.

"Yeah, and I called. Twice." Mel's voice was tinged with frustration and worry, a cocktail of emotions that seemed to be the drink du jour at Club MIILFF lately. "Yesterday, she called me three times. I texted her that I was busy drafting a scene, and she said she really needed to talk to me. We made plans to meet for coffee, and she just... vanished."

Leah's frown deepened, etching lines into her usually smooth forehead. "Maddie? Miss Punctuality herself? That's weird."

"I know, right?" Mel agreed, her emerald eyes clouded with concern. "It's like she's fallen off the face of the earth. Poof! Gone with the wind but without the fancy curtain dress."

Leah's mind flashed back to when Maddie first joined Club MIILFF. The memory unfurled like a time-lapse video of a flower blooming. Maddie had been a struggling single mom, barely making ends meet, her designer dreams limited to window shopping and wistful sighs. But with the club's resources, she put herself through nursing school, burning the midnight oil while juggling diapers and textbooks.

When Maddie realized she could take care of her child and still pick up night shifts as a nurse, she began spreading the word to her friends like it was the hottest gossip at a PTA meeting. Before long, she was recruiting nurses left and right. Her enthusiasm, as infectious as her bedside manner, was comforting.

With Club MIILFF's backing, Maddie founded Prime Nursing Care, which quickly became the number two staffing agency in the tri-state area. When Mel's sister had a baby, Prime Care staffed the baby nurse, solidifying Mel and Maddie's friendship for life. It was like something out of a Hallmark movie - if Hallmark ever decided to do a series on glamorous, entrepreneurial moms.

Leah shook herself out of her reverie, the present situation demanding her full attention. "Did you try her assistant?"

Mel nodded, exasperated. "Dead end. It's like she vanished into thin air. Poof! Gone with the wind, again, but without the fancy curtain dress."

As if summoned by their concern, Meryl's statuesque form appeared at the end of the hallway, her Hermès scarf trailing behind her like a cape. She moved with the grace of a gazelle and the purpose of a lioness on the hunt. Ivanka followed close behind, her stilettos clicking in perfect sync with her mother's, a well-choreographed dance of power and poise.

"Ladies," Meryl called out, her voice carrying effortlessly down the marble corridor, smooth as aged whiskey and twice as intoxicating. "Gather 'round. We need to talk."

Leah and Mel exchanged worried glances, a silent conversation passing between them in the blink of an eye, before following Meryl and Ivanka into the conference room. The space buzzed with tension, thick enough to cut with a diamond-encrusted letter opener.

The other MIILFFs filed in, each a vision of success and carefully curated style. Krystal Kream, ever the picture of flamboyant excess, perched on her ergonomic chair like an exotic bird ready to take flight. Her bedazzled glasses glinted in the chandelier light, throwing tiny rainbows across the glossy table.

"You know the drill," Krystal drawled, sliding an iPad across the table with the nonchalance of someone passing the salt. "Weekly signatures here!"

Leah's eyebrows furrowed as she picked up the stylus, its weight suddenly feeling like that of Atlas's burden. "Don't you think it's a bit much, signing fresh NDAs every week?"

Krystal snapped her gum, the sound echoing in the tense room like a starter pistol at a race no one was sure they wanted to run. "I dunno, Ms. Corporate Minute. Do you want your private business out there in the public? Because let me tell you, honey, the paparazzi would have a field day with half the stuff that goes on in here."

Leah hesitated, her stylus hovering over the screen like a hummingbird unsure which flower to choose. It's not like she had anything to hide, but still... The uneasy feeling in her gut grew, transforming from a whisper to a full-blown shout.

"Alright, spill the tea," Natasha demanded, setting down her kiwi-strawberry vape with a dramatic flourish that would have made Shakespeare proud. A cloud of fruity-scented vapor swirled around her expertly highlighted hair, creating a halo effect that was both angelic and slightly ridiculous. "Where's our little Maddy Madds?"

Meryl's face was a mask of practiced concern as she took her place at the head of the table, every movement calculated for maximum impact. "I'm afraid I have some... unsettling news." She paused for effect, her gaze sweeping across the room like a searchlight, pinning each MIILFF in place. "Maddie has decided to step down from Prime Nursing Care. Effective immediately."

A chorus of gasps and "What the hells?" erupted around the table, the cacophony of shock and disbelief rising like a tide. Leah felt like she'd been punched in the gut by a heavyweight champion wearing brass knuckles.

"Step down?" she interjected, her voice rising like a balloon released into the air. "But Prime Nursing was her baby! She wouldn't just abandon it without a word. That's like... like leaving your Birkin in a taxi!"

Ivanka, who had been silent until now, slid a stack of papers across the glossy table. Her manicured nails tapped a staccato rhythm on the document's cover, a beat that sounded suspiciously like a funeral march. "It's all here in black and white, ladies. Maddie signed over her shares and leadership. Everything's above board."

Krystal squinted at the documents, pushing her bedazzled glasses further up her nose as if the extra millimeter would suddenly make the legalese crystal clear. "Oy vey, this legalese gives me a migraine. Can someone translate these Mishigas into English? Or at least into something less... lawyer-y?"

"It means," Ivanka said coolly, her tone at odds with the warmth of her honey-blonde highlights, "that Prime Nursing Care is now under new management. Specifically, under the MIILFF umbrella corporation."

Natasha's eyes narrowed, her vape forgotten, the fruity cloud dissipating like their illusions of control. "And Maddie agreed to this? Just like that? What, did she get abducted by aliens and replaced with a pod person?"

Meryl's smile was tight, her botox-smoothed forehead betraying no emotion. It was like trying to read the expressions of a particularly glamorous statue. "Sometimes, the reality is, the pressures of success can be... overwhelming. Maddie felt it was best to step back. Let's not forget, she was very young. Maybe she just wasn't ready for this kind of responsibility." She shrugged her shoulders effortlessly, the movement causing her designer scarf to shimmer in the light like a mirage in the desert of truth.

"Now," Meryl continued, her voice taking on a more upbeat tone that felt as genuine as a three-dollar bill, "who wants to hear about our exciting new expansion plans? We have some new MIILFFs joining, and they are really looking forward to your support! I'm sure many of you remember what it was like to be a newbie. And now, you can pay it forward with our new MIILFFs as you continue to embrace what being a true MIILFF is. A mother interested in launching Financial Freedom!"

Mel's face tensed up, a flicker of uncertainty crossing her features faster than a New York minute. Did anyone else know she wasn't a mother? The secret felt like a ticking time bomb in her designer clutch.

As Meryl launched into a dazzling presentation, complete with holographic projections of smiling nurses and the idea of virtual visits that looked like something out of a sci-fi blockbuster, Leah couldn't shake the unease settling in her stomach. It felt like she'd swallowed a gallon of her green juice smoothie, but without any of the alleged health benefits.

She leaned over to Mel, whispering, "Does this feel off to you? Like, 'wearing white after Labor Day' levels of wrong?"

Mel nodded slightly, her eyes never leaving Meryl. "Like an oddly written novel. But, with all this money rolling in... and our success, I just... I don't know. It's like we're living in a golden cage, and I can't tell if we're the birds or the zookeepers."

"I know," Leah sighed. "It's confusing... I'm confused. It's like trying to solve a Rubik's cube blindfolded while riding a unicycle."

The meeting continued, with Meryl outlining ambitious plans for global domination in the world of mommy millionaires. But Leah found it hard to focus, her mind constantly drifting back to Maddie's sudden disappearance. It was like trying to watch a blockbuster movie while someone was whispering spoilers in your ear.

As the MIILFFs filed out of the conference room, Leah pulled Mel aside, her grip on Mel's arm tighter than a pair of Spanx two sizes too small. "We need to talk. Meet me at The Little Latte in an hour?"

Mel nodded, her eyes darting around to make sure no one was listening. "I'll be there. And I'll bring my invisible ink pen, just in case."

An hour later, Leah sat in a secluded corner of The Little Latte, a trendy coffee shop that catered to the MIILFF crowd. The walls were adorned with motivational quotes in rose gold lettering, each one more vapid than the last. The air was thick with the scent of artisanal coffee beans and success, with a hint of desperation lingering just beneath the surface.

Mel slid into the seat across from her, clutching a matcha latte like it was the last lifeboat on the Titanic. "Okay, spill. What's going on in that beautiful, calculating brain of yours? And please tell me it's more exciting than the PTA bake sale drama."

Leah leaned in, her voice low enough to make a librarian proud. "Something's not right, Mel. Maddie wouldn't just leave like this. It's like expecting Anna Wintour to show up at Fashion Week in Crocs. And those weekly NDAs? I did some digging. They're not standard practice, even for high-level executives. It's fishier than the sushi bar at that sketchy all-you-can-eat buffet."

Mel's eyes widened, her latte forgotten. "You think there's something sinister going on? Like, 'made-for-TV movie' sinister or 'call the FBI' sinister?"

"I don't know," Leah admitted, stirring her oat milk cappuccino absently, creating a miniature whirlpool of froth and uncertainty. "But I think we need to start asking some serious questions. The kind of questions that make people squirm more than a toddler in timeout."

Just then, Huvi sauntered up to their table, her statuesque form drawing admiring glances from around the cafe. She moved with the confidence of a woman who knew she could stop traffic with a single raised eyebrow. "Mind if I join you, darlings? I couldn't help but overhear, and I think I might have some information that could help. Plus, this corner has the best lighting for selfies."

Leah and Mel exchanged glances before nodding. Huvi settled into a chair, her designer dress rustling softly, like money whispering secrets.

"Now," Huvi began, her voice low and conspiratorial, leaning in so close they could smell her Chanel No. 5, "I may be new to the MIILFF game, but I've been around the block a few times. And let me tell you, something smells fishier than that chic I hooked up with last week."

Silence descended upon the table like a heavy velvet curtain.

"No really, what the heck do you mean?" Mel asked, leaning in so far she was practically lying on the table. "And please, spare us the details of your... extracurricular activities."

Huvi's perfectly arched eyebrow rose, a feat of muscular control that would impress any Pilates instructor. "Well, darling, let's just say I've seen my fair share of corporate takeovers in my time. And this? This has all the hallmarks of a hostile one. It's like 'The Devil Wears Prada' meets 'Wall Street,' but with more Botox and better shoes."

Leah felt a chill run down her spine, colder than the iced latte she'd left forgotten on the table. "But why? We're all successful already. Why would Meryl and Ivanka need to take over? It's not like they're short on Hermès scarves and power suits."

"Power, honey," Huvi said, her long nails tapping a rhythm on the table that sounded suspiciously like the theme from 'Jaws.' "It's not about the money anymore. It's about control. They want to be the puppet masters, and we're all just Gucci-clad marionettes dancing to their tune."

The three women sat in silence for a moment, the gravity of the situation settling over them like a designer throw blanket – beautiful, but with an underlying scratchy discomfort.

"So, what do we do?" Mel finally asked, her voice barely above a whisper. "Start a support group? 'Millionaires Anonymous: For When Success Becomes a Cage'?"

Leah's jaw set with determination, her expression reminiscent of a general about to lead troops into battle – if the troops wore stilettos and the battlefield was a boardroom. "We investigate. We find Maddie. And we get to the bottom of this. It's time to put our MIILFF skills to use for something other than Instagram-worthy lunch meetings."

As they left The Little Latte, a plan forming between them like a complex braid of ambition, fear, and righteous indignation, none of them noticed the sleek black car parked across the street. Its tinted windows concealed the occupant, who watched their every move with the intensity of a fashion critic at a runway show.

Weeks passed, and the absence of Maddie became a fading memory, replaced by the intoxicating rush of success that flowed through Club MIILFF like a river of champagne. Prime Nursing Care was expanding faster than a pregnant woman's waistline, with new contracts pouring in daily. Mel's screenplay was a hit, and producers were already reaching out for follow-ups, treating her like the second coming of Nora Ephron. Leah was starting her own podcast, "MIILFF Money Moves," which was climbing the charts faster than a toddler on a sugar high chasing an ice cream truck.

But beneath the surface of their glossy success, Leah and Mel continued their quiet investigation, feeling like a pair of Prada-clad Nancy Drews. They combed through financial records with the intensity of bargain hunters at a sample sale, reached out to old contacts as if networking for the most exclusive party in town, and tried to piece together the puzzle of Maddie's disappearance like it was the world's most frustrating jigsaw.

Then, on a rainy Tuesday morning that seemed to mirror the gloomy mood settling over Club MIILFF, it happened again.

Leah burst into Mel's office, her face paler than a socialite who'd just run out of self-tanner. Her usually perfect blow-out was slightly frizzed from the humidity, making her look like she'd just walked off the set of a shampoo commercial gone wrong. "Reese is gone," she announced, her voice a mix of dread and disbelief.

Mel looked up from her spreadsheets, her reading glasses perched precariously on the end of her nose like a diver about to take the plunge. "Gone shopping? That girl does love her retail therapy. Remember when she bought out half of Bergdorf's because she was 'having a bad hair day'?"

Leah shook her head, her voice dropping to an urgent whisper that would make any conspiracy theorist proud. "No, gone gone. Like Maddie. Vanished. Poof. Her whole product line has been absorbed into the MIILFF brand faster than you can say 'hostile takeover.' Her social media managers and her content creators are all reporting to Ivanka now. It's like Reese never existed."

A chill ran through the room, colder than a high-end cryotherapy session gone wrong. Mel's voice dropped to match Leah's whisper, the two of them huddled together like kids sharing secrets at a slumber party. "What the hell is going on here? First Maddie, now

Reese? It's like we're in some twisted version of 'And Then There Were None,' but with designer handbags and power suits."

"I don't know," Leah replied, her voice trembling like a leaf in a hurricane. "But I'm starting to think our little club might have a dark side. It's less 'Sex and the City' and more 'American Psycho' – but with better shoes."

Just then, Natasha poked her head in, a cloud of cotton candy vape smoke preceding her like a sweet-smelling harbinger of doom. "Hey, boss babes," she chirped, her voice as artificially cheery as her hair color, "Meryl's calling an emergency meeting." She took a long drag on her vape, then frowned as if she'd just discovered a scuff on her Louboutins. "Crap, my battery died. These vapes are garbage! Anyway, she says she has big news about the future of Club MIILFF. Sounds ominous, right? Like, 'winter is coming' levels of ominous."

As they made their way to the conference room, the click of their heels on marble felt more ominous than empowering, like a count-down to something they weren't sure they wanted to face. The chan-delier light, once warm and inviting, now cast long shadows across the faces of the remaining MIILFFs, turning the hallway into a catwalk of concern.

Meryl stood at the head of the table, resplendent in a power suit that probably cost more than most people's cars. Her smile was dazzling, but her eyes were cold, like diamonds – beautiful, hard, and poten-tially cutting.

"Ladies," she began, her voice smooth as expensive silk and twice as slippery, "I have a feeling this is going to be our best fiscal year yet. We are killing it. Each one of you has been an incredibly successful business leader this year. And today, I want to reward you." Her words dripped with honey, but there was an underlying bitterness that made Leah's stomach churn.

She waved towards One, who quickly motioned to other similar ones. In unison, they click-clacked towards each MIILFF with a gift box in hand, moving with the precision of a well-oiled machine – or perhaps, more accurately, a group of very well-dressed robots.

Natasha didn't waste a moment, tearing into the box like a kid on Christmas morning – if that kid were a grown woman with a penchant for luxury goods and questionable decision-making skills. "Staaaap," she purred, her voice a mixture of delight and affected nonchalance. "A tennis bracelet from Harry Winston!" she shrieked with delight, her excitement palpable enough to power a small city.

Krystal put hers on immediately, the diamonds catching the light and throwing tiny rainbows across the room. "I am never taking this off!" she declared, admiring her wrist as if it had just been bestowed with superpowers instead of overpriced jewelry.

Mel eyed Leah, neither one of them touching their bracelets. The boxes sat in front of them like Pandora's own jewelry collection, beautiful and potentially catastrophic.

Meryl smiled, proud of herself, like a cat who'd not only got the cream but had managed to buy out the entire dairy. "Now, MIILFFs, who is ready to talk about our global expansion plans?" Her voice dripped with excitement, but to Leah's ears, it sounded more like a predator luring its prey.

As Meryl's voice filled the room with promises of wealth, gifts, success, and power, Leah caught Mel's eye again. In that moment, they both knew: the price of their financial freedom might be higher than they ever imagined. It was like they'd signed up for a luxury cruise and found themselves on the Titanic instead.

Later that evening, Leah, Mel, and Layla met in Leah's dimly lit living room. The blank TV loomed in the background like a silent witness to their clandestine meeting, its dark screen reflecting their serious expressions.

"Okay," Leah said, spreading out a series of documents on the table with the precision of a general planning a battle strategy. "Here's what we know. Maddie and Reese are both gone, vanished like last season's trends. Their companies have been absorbed into the MIILFF brand faster than you can say 'corporate takeover.' And these weekly 'NDAs' we've been signing? They're not NDAs at all. They're about as much NDAs as I am a natural blonde."

Mel leaned in, her brow furrowed deeper than the Mariana Trench. "What are they, then? Some kind of magical contract that turns pumpkins into carriages and MIILFFs into corporate slaves?"

Huvi, who had been examining the papers with the intensity of a jeweler inspecting a suspect diamond, looked up, her expression grim. "They're transfer of ownership agreements. Every week, we've been signing away a little piece of our companies. It's like we're in a really messed up version of 'The Little Mermaid,' except instead of our voices, we're giving away our businesses."

The silence that followed was deafening, thick enough to cut with a diamond-encrusted letter opener. Finally, Mel spoke, her voice barely above a whisper, as if afraid the walls themselves might be listening. "So, what do we do now? Start a support group for ex-MIILFFs? 'Hello, my name is Mel, and I'm a recovering millionaire mom'?"

Leah's jaw set with determination, her expression reminiscent of a general about to lead troops into battle – if the troops wore stilettos and the battlefield was a boardroom. "We fight back. We find Maddie and Reese. And we take back what's ours. It's time to show Meryl and Ivanka that hell hath no fury like a MIILFF scorned."

Huvi nodded, a mischievous glint in her eye that would make any cat burglar proud. "I might know someone who can help. An old friend from my... less glamorous days. He's a whiz with computers. If there's a digital trail, he can find it. Think of him as our own personal Sherlock Holmes, but with better hair and a keyboard instead of a magnifying glass."

As they formulated their plan, bouncing ideas off each other like a high-stakes game of verbal tennis, none of them noticed the small, blinking light in the corner of the room. It pulsed quietly, a silent sentinel broadcasting their every word to unseen ears.

In a sleek office across town, a space that screamed 'evil lair' but with better interior design, Meryl and Ivanka watched the feed, their expressions as unreadable as a blank check.

"They're catching on," Ivanka said, her voice neutral, as if commenting on the weather rather than a potential uprising in their carefully crafted empire.

Meryl nodded, taking a sip of her martini with the casual elegance of a woman who had the world on a string – and liked to pull it tight. "I see," she murmured, her tone giving away nothing.

Ivanka paused, a flicker of something – doubt? Concern? – crossing her features. "Mom... maybe it's enough. We have enough." The words hung in the air, fragile as a soap bubble and potentially just as easy to burst.

Meryl remained silent, the ice in her glass clinking softly as she swirled her drink, the sound echoing in the tense quiet of the room.

Ivanka came over to the other side of the desk to hug her mother, the gesture both affectionate and slightly desperate. "We can end this now, Mom, before it's too late. Before we cross a line we can't come back from."

Suddenly, her phone rang, shattering the moment like a stiletto through a sheet of ice. Ivanka looked at the caller ID and rolled her eyes, the mundane intrusion of real life a stark contrast to the high-stakes drama unfolding around them. "Ugh, it's the P.T.A. I have to deal with ridiculous committee votes for flavors of ice cream. I gotta go!" She walked up to the door, turned around and said solemnly, "Mom, just think about it. We're not the villains in some made-for-TV movie. We don't have to be."

As Ivanka's footsteps faded away, Meryl remained alone in her office, a queen surveying her kingdom from her glass and steel tower. She picked up her glass, took a deep swig, and muttered, her words barely audible in the empty room, "Oh, Ivanka, if only the choice were up to me."

The words hung in the air, heavy with implication, as Meryl turned back to the screens, watching the MIILFFs plot their resistance. The chess pieces were in motion, and the game was far from over. In the world of Club MIILFF, it seemed the price of success might be steeper than anyone had bargained for.

CHAPTER SEVENTEEN
EXIT PLAN

Love me… Love me like you do
Touch me like you do
What are you waiting for?
After all these years, Leah, you are still jealous!!!
Shame on you
Hey, Stop it
It's ok.
You are human.
Love me like you do.
She does love you doesn't she?
You are so lucky to be loved by that woman.

Mimi stood at the floor-to-ceiling windows of her penthouse apartment, absently twirling a glass of chardonnay. The delicate stem felt fragile between her fingers, much like her current state of mind. The New York skyline sprawled before her, a glittering testament to ambition and success. Her success. Yet as the sun dipped below the horizon, painting the sky in hues of pink and gold that would make any wedding planner swoon, Mimi felt a hollowness that no amount of achievement – or alcohol – could fill.

"I DO, huh," she murmured, a wry smile playing on her lips. The words, once a powerful mantra that had built her empire, now felt hollow, echoing in the vast emptiness of her luxurious apartment. The empire she'd built, the legacy she'd crafted – it was all she'd ever wanted. Wasn't it? The question hung in the air, heavier than the designer curtains framing her million-dollar view.

Her gaze fell on a framed photo on the nearby console table, its silver frame catching the last rays of the setting sun. It was from the last Club MIILFF gala, all of them dressed to the nines, champagne flutes in hand, success and ambition radiating from every perfectly styled hair. Leah, with her shrewd business acumen hidden behind a megawatt smile. Natasha, flamboyant and unapologetic, her arm slung around a laughing Maddie. And then there was Mel. Mimi's heart did a little flip as her eyes lingered on Mel's face, that crooked smile that always seemed to hint at some private joke, those eyes that sparkled with mischief and something deeper, something Mimi had never dared to name.

With a sigh that seemed to come from the depths of her Louboutin-clad soul, Mimi moved to her plush sofa, sinking into its embrace like it was the only thing holding her up. She picked up her phone, its screen dark and accusing. Her thumb hovered over Mel's contact, the familiar profile picture making her heart race in a way that had nothing to do with too much wine. How many times had she almost called? How many drafted messages sat unsent, each word agonized over like a prenup for a billionaire's fourth marriage?

"Get it together, Mimi," she chided herself, her voice echoing in the empty apartment. "She's just a friend. Was just a friend." The words tasted bitter, like day-old coffee or the lies she'd been telling herself.

But even as the words left her lips, she knew they weren't true. Mel had been more than just a friend. She'd been a confidante, a partner in crime, a source of laughter and light in the often cutthroat world of Club MIILFF. Mel had been the one person who saw beyond the perfectly curated image of Mimi, the Wedding Empire Queen, to the woman underneath – with all her doubts, fears, and secret longings.

Mimi closed her eyes, letting the memories wash over her like a wave of expensive perfume. Late nights brainstorming ideas for I DO's expansion, their excitement palpable as they dreamed up bigger and bolder plans. Inside jokes about Natasha's outrageous schemes, giggling like schoolgirls over a particularly audacious plan involving flamingos and the Statue of Liberty. The way Mel's eyes would light up when she talked about her writing, her dreams, her vision for the future – a passion that Mimi found both inspiring and terrifyingly attractive.

Had it been love? Mimi wasn't sure. Love was for fairytales and the weddings she orchestrated, not for hard-nosed businesswomen who had empires to run. All she knew was that now, months after leaving Club MIILFF behind, it was Mel she missed the most. Mel's sarcastic quips could cut through any boardroom tension, her unwavering support when a big deal fell through, her ability to see through Mimi's carefully constructed façade to the woman underneath – the woman who sometimes just wanted to kick off her heels and eat ice cream straight from the carton.

"I should call her," Mimi said to the empty room, her voice small and uncertain. But she didn't move. Couldn't move. Because calling Mel meant facing questions, she wasn't ready to answer. About why she'd left. About what really happened in those final days at Club MIILFF. About the feelings that swirled in her chest every time she thought of Mel's smile.

The truth was something had felt off for a while. Little things at first – whispered conversations that stopped when she entered a room, leaving an awkward silence in their wake. Documents hastily shoved into drawers, the rustling of papers like guilty confessions.

Cryptic messages on phones quickly turned face-down, leaving Mimi to wonder what secrets were being kept.

The larger discrepancies started to appear, like cracks in the foundation of a seemingly perfect wedding venue. Numbers that didn't add up, no matter how many times she ran them. Deals that seemed too good to be true, with fine print that made her skin crawl. Connections that felt... unsavory, like the lingering aftertaste of a bad champagne.

Mimi took a large swig of her wine, trying to drown out the nagging voice in her head. She'd tried to ignore it, to rationalize it away. After all, Club MIILFF had given her everything – success, wealth, a platform to help other women achieve their dreams. How could something that did so much good be... wrong? It was like questioning the authenticity of a diamond – you didn't want to look too closely for fear of finding a flaw.

But the feeling had persisted, growing stronger with each passing day. Until finally, she couldn't ignore it anymore. The weight of her suspicions, her fears, her unnamed dread had become too heavy to bear. She'd left abruptly, like a runaway bride fleeing the altar. She'd spoken to no one, not even Mel. Especially not Mel. Because looking into those warm, understanding eyes might have broken her resolve completely.

Now, she was cut off from the sisterhood that had been her lifeline, her family. The other MIILFFs, with their shared dreams and ambitions, their inside jokes and secret handshakes. And Mel. Always Mel, at the forefront of her thoughts, the one loose end she couldn't seem to tie up neatly.

Mimi's phone buzzed, startling her out of her reverie. The screen lit up, Mel's name flashing like a beacon in the darkening room. A text: "See you tomorrow? Can't wait to catch up. Miss you, my work wife! "

Before Mimi could even think, her thumb moved of its own accord, muscle memory taking over. She hit 'Yes,' her heart racing at the thought of seeing Mel again.

"Why did you hit yes, dummy?" she muttered to herself, the familiar self-recrimination creeping in. But she knew why. It was so easy to say yes. To slip back into that world of power and privilege, of shared secrets and ambitious dreams. To see Mel again, to bask in the warmth of her smile, to pretend for a moment that everything was fine, that she hadn't uncovered something rotten at the core of their glittering world.

But the unease stirred in her gut, that nameless dread that had driven her away in the first place. Something wasn't right at Club MIILFF. Something lurked beneath the surface, behind the empowering slogans and feel-good success stories. Something dark and insidious, like a shadow creeping across a perfectly manicured lawn.

Mimi set her phone down without replying further, her finger hovering over the option to unsend her hasty 'Yes.' She stood, moving back to the window, drawn to the vista like a moth to a flame. The city lights twinkled, each one a story, a life, a dream. Somewhere out there, she hoped Mel was living her life, writing her stories, probably wondering why Mimi had disappeared without a real goodbye. The thought of Mel's confusion and her hurt was almost enough to make Mimi pick up the phone again.

"I'm sorry, Mel," Mimi whispered to the night sky, her breath fogging the glass. "I'm sorry I couldn't tell you. I'm sorry, I still can't." The words felt inadequate, like trying to fix a broken heart with a Band-Aid.

As she stood there, caught between the life she'd left behind and the uncertain future ahead, Mimi made a silent promise to herself. One day, she'd find the courage to face the truth – about Club MIILFF, about her feelings for Mel, about who she really was beneath the successful entrepreneur persona she'd crafted as carefully as any wedding bouquet.

One day, she'd call Mel and tell her everything. About the longing that kept her awake at night, the fear that churned in her stomach every time she thought of what she'd discovered. About the suspicions that plagued her, the doubts that clouded every memory of their time together in Club MIILFF. About the depth of her feelings, the breadth of her regrets, the way Mel's smile could light up even her darkest days.

But not tonight. Tonight, she would sit with her memories, her doubts, her unnamed fears. She'd nurse her glass of wine and try to ignore the way her finger itched to dial Mel's number to hear her voice one more time.

And tomorrow... tomorrow, she would wake up and continue to build her empire, one perfectly planned wedding at a time. She'd paste on her professional smile, the one that never quite reached her eyes these days, and she'd make more brides' dreams come true because that's what MIILFFs did. They persevered. They succeeded. They kept their secrets.

Even when those secrets threatened to tear them apart.

Mimi raised her glass in a silent toast to the city, to the life she'd built, to the woman she used to be. "Here's to you, Mel," she murmured. "To what might have been. To what can never be."

As the last light faded from the sky, Mimi turned away from the window. She had a wedding to plan, an empire to run, and secrets to keep. The loneliness of her penthouse settled around her like a familiar cloak as she prepared to face another day of smiles, success, and silent regrets.

Chapter Eighteen
Queens

Welcome to the Queendom
It's a holy sanctuary
Make a blessing on my body
Cause I find it necessary in the Queendom
Hips. Stretch.
Some days, I really feel like a queen
I feel sexy and graceful and pretty.
And some days I feel like a saggy Rugeleh with extra rolls

Leah sat at her desk in the Club MIILFF office, the bustle of the day fading as evening settled over the city. The Manhattan skyline glittered beyond her window, a tapestry of ambition and dreams woven in steel and glass. She should have left hours ago, but something kept her rooted to her ergonomic chair, lost in thought. Her fingers absently traced the edge of a framed photo on her desk - a candid shot of her and Jack, both laughing, taken at last year's MIILFF summer picnic. The memory of that day, filled with sunshine and hope, seemed to glow from within the silver frame.

"How far we've come," Leah murmured, her voice barely a whisper in the quiet office.

She closed her eyes, letting the memories wash over her like a bitter-sweet tide. It seemed like a lifetime ago, but the pain was still there, a dull ache that never quite went away, like a phantom limb of her former life.

The fear came rushing back, the constant walking on eggshells in her own home. Her ex-husband's rage his threats, echoed in her mind with haunting clarity. "I'll ruin you," he'd snarled, his breath hot with alcohol and hatred. "I'll tell everyone at your job what a whore you are. I'll tell the whole community how you've betrayed us all."

Leah shuddered, her arms instinctively wrapping around herself as if to ward off the memory. She remembered how she'd believed him, how she'd stayed silent for so long, her voice locked away like a bird in a gilded cage. The Ultra-Orthodox community had been her whole world, a tapestry of tradition and faith that she'd been woven into since birth. The thought of losing it, of being cast out, had terri-fied her more than the bruises that bloomed like dark flowers on her skin.

But then came the day she found out about her child's addiction. The little bags were hidden in stuffed animals, the lies that fell from once-innocent lips, and the late nights of worry that etched lines into her face. Her bright, beautiful child was hollowed out by heroin, a shadow of the vibrant soul she'd brought into the world. It had nearly broken Leah, splintering her heart into a thousand jagged pieces.

"Why didn't you notice?" her husband had raged, his words sharp as broken glass. "What kind of mother are you?"

Those words had been the final straw, the spark that ignited the inferno of her resolve. Because in that moment, Leah realized - she was a damn good mother. A mother who'd do anything for her child.

Including leaving everything she'd ever known behind and stepping out into a world as unfamiliar as a foreign country.

The rehab had been hell, a crucible of pain and hope. Watching her child struggle, hearing the cries in the night that echoed her own silent screams. Taking ownership of the chaotic mess her child was exposed to, and knowing she had no power but to let chaos hit before rebuilding. The conversations replayed in her mind, each word a step on the path to healing.

"You were cruel," Leah said.

"I was. I am so sorry." Jack meant it.

"You really hurt me," her child had said, voice raw with emotion.

"I did. I'm sorry," Leah had replied, her heart breaking anew.

"You made me feel abandoned."

"I did. I'm sorry."

But slowly, painfully, they'd found their way back to each other. They'd discovered the gift of just being, of existing in the same space without expectations or judgment. And, in moments of levity that felt like miracles, they'd rediscovered laughter over shared slices of pizza.

They'd made it through. Together.

Leah opened her eyes, the present rushing back in like a wave. She glanced at her watch, realizing with a start that it was well past time to head home. As she gathered her things, a smile played on her lips. Tomorrow was another day, another chance to be the woman - and the mother - she'd fought so hard to become.

Welcome to the Queendom.

The lyrics of an empowering anthem echoed in Leah's mind as she made her way to the MIILFF conference room the next morning.

"It's a holy sanctuary. Make a blessing on my body 'Cause I find it necessary in the Queendom."

Her hips swayed slightly to the imaginary beat, a private dance of confidence and self-assurance. As she pushed open the door, the familiar cacophony of pre-meeting chatter washed over her like a warm embrace.

The MIILFF conference room hummed with energy, a symphony of clicking heels and clinking jewelry orchestrating the usual pre-weekly meeting bustle. The air was thick with a heady mixture of designer perfumes and ambition, with just a hint of freshly brewed coffee cutting through it all.

Leah sauntered in, her stride confident and relaxed, grande latte in hand. She plopped down next to Mel, the leather chair sighing softly beneath her.

"So," Leah whispered, leaning in conspiratorially, her eyes sparkling with curiosity, "heard anything about this new member? I'm dying for some juicy intel."

Mel shrugged, her eyes never leaving her phone as her thumbs danced across the screen with practiced precision. "Nada. But rumor has it she's opening some kind of club. Very hush-hush, very exclusive."

"Ooh, like a book club?" Krystal chimed in, her bedazzled glasses sliding down her nose as she perked up. The rhinestones caught the light, sending tiny rainbows dancing across the polished table. "I've got a stack of steamy novels just begging for a dramatic reading. You haven't lived until you've heard me do the voices."

Natasha snorted, a plume of strawberry kiwi vape escaping her nostrils like a fruity dragon. "Please, the last thing we need is you dramatically reading about throbbing members and heaving bosoms. Some of us are trying to maintain our professional dignity here."

"Oh honey," Krystal retorted, pushing her glasses back up with a perfectly manicured finger, "if you think dignity and a good bodice-ripper are mutually exclusive, you're not reading the right books."

"Ladies, ladies!" Meryl's voice cut through the chatter like a Givenchy-clad knife, silencing the room with the practiced ease of a seasoned CEO. All eyes turned to her as she stood at the head of the table, radiating authority and impeccable style in equal measure. "Let's all welcome our newest MIILFF, Laverne!"

The atmosphere in the room shifted, curiosity and anticipation crackling like static electricity. All heads turned as Laverne strode in, six feet of pure confidence perched atop stilettos that could double as lethally weapons. Her entrance was nothing short of cinematic – if Busby Berkeley had choreographed power moves instead of dance numbers.

Laverne's smile was dazzling, bright enough to rival the chandeliers overhead. Her handshake, as she made her way around the table, was firm and warm, each greeting accompanied by a look that made everyone feel like the most fascinating person in the room.

"Hello, darlings," Laverne purred, her voice a rich contralto that seemed to caress each syllable. "I'm absolutely thrilled to be here. You know what they say - if you can't beat 'em, join 'em... and then beat 'em at their own game." She winked, the gesture somehow both conspiratorial and challenging.

Natasha's eyes narrowed, her vape forgotten as she leaned forward, elbows on the table. "And what game is that, exactly? We're not exactly running a social club here, honey. This is serious business."

Laverne's grin widened, a Cheshire cat with secrets to spare. "Why, the art of the tease, of course. I'm opening 'The Gilded Tassel,' the most exclusive gentleman's club on this side of the Atlantic. New York has seen honey, but it's never seen anything quite like this."

A hush fell over the room, broken only by the sound of Krystal choking on her chamomile tea. Mel pounded her on the back as Krystal spluttered, "Did she say, 'gentleman's club'? As in, strippers and poles and... and... glitter?"

"I'm sorry," Natasha drawled, her tone dripping with skepticism, "but isn't this supposed to be a group for mothers? Last I checked it required certain equipment. You know, the kind that pushes out babies, not dollar bills into G-strings."

Laverne's smile never faltered, her poise unshakeable in the face of Natasha's pointed remark. "Oh honey," she said, her voice warm but with an edge of steel beneath the velvet, "motherhood isn't about equipment. It's about love, nurture, and the ability to rock a kick-ass pair of heels while juggling a career and family. Besides," she added with a wink, "my two rescue pugs are basically fur babies. You haven't known true maternal sacrifice until you've cleaned up pug drool from silk sheets at 3 AM."

Leah snorted into her latte, a mixture of amusement and admiration dancing in her eyes. "Fur babies? Girl, you'll fit right in. We've got more varieties of motherhood in this room than Baskin Robbins has flavors."

Meryl clapped her hands, the sharp sound cutting through the mix of giggles and murmurs. Her expression was all business, but there was a glimmer of approval in her eyes as she regarded Laverne. "Alright, let's get down to brass tacks. Or should I say, golden tassels? Laverne, walk us through your business plan. I want details projections, and don't skimp on the glitter."

As Laverne launched into her presentation, complete with vivid holographic projections of tastefully designed interiors that managed to be both sultry and sophisticated, Natasha leaned over to Mel, her voice a heated whisper.

"This is ridiculous," she hissed, gesturing towards Laverne with her vape pen. "What's next? We start letting in anyone with a pulse and a pipe dream. I thought we had standards."

Mel shifted uncomfortably, her eyes darting between Natasha and Laverne. "I don't know," she murmured, her voice tinged with uncertainty. "She seems pretty savvy. And it's not like all of us are traditional moms..."

Natasha's eyebrows shot up, disappearing beneath her expertly styled bangs. "What's that supposed to mean? Are you saying I'm not a real mother because I have a nanny and a personal chef?"

Before Mel could respond, her mouth opening and closing like a fish out of water, Krystal's voice rang out, cutting through the tension like a bedazzled knife.

"Hold up, hold up!" Krystal exclaimed, waving her hand in the air like an enthusiastic student. "I've got a question for our newbie. How exactly does one gild a tassel? Is it like a spray paint situation or more of a dipping process? Asking for a friend, of course." She giggled, the sound tinkling like the crystal chandelier above.

Laverne laughed, the sound rich and genuine. "Trade secret, darling. But I'll tell you this - it involves a lot of body glitter and a little bit of magic." She winked, adding with a smirk, "And maybe a dash of industrial-strength adhesive. A lady never reveals all her secrets, but I will say this – what happens at The Gilded Tassel stays at The Gilded Tassel. Unless, of course, it ends up on Page Six."

As the meeting wrapped up, the room buzzing with a mixture of excitement and trepidation, Meryl pulled Mel aside. Her touch was gentle but firm, guiding Mel to a quiet corner of the room.

"Everything okay, dear?" Meryl asked, her voice low and concerned. "You seemed a bit... off today. Like a Louboutin with a broken heel – still fabulous, but not quite steady."

Mel sighed, her shoulders slumping slightly. "It's just... all this talk about motherhood. I mean, I'm not exactly..." She trailed off, unable to voice the thought that had been gnawing at her.

"A mother?" Meryl finished, her voice gentle but matter of fact. "Oh, honey. Being a MIILFF isn't about biology. It's about spirit. You've got more maternal instinct in your little finger than some people have in their whole body. Remember how you nursed that screenplay of yours from a random idea scribbled on a cocktail napkin to a blockbuster hit? That's creativity and nurturing at its finest."

Mel couldn't help but smile, a small chuckle escaping her lips. "I did lose a lot of sleep over that baby. Probably more than I would have with a real one – at least kids eventually sleep through the night."

"Exactly!" Meryl exclaimed, giving Mel's shoulder a supportive squeeze. "Now, let's go show these ladies what a real MIILFF is made of. Spoiler alert: it's 90% caffeine, 10% pure, unadulterated sass, and 100% heart." She paused, her voice dropping to a conspiratorial whisper, "Mel, this club is about reclaiming a word that has been used against us and repackaging it in a way that leaves us with control over the narrative. We're not victims or objects – we're the authors of our own stories."

Mel's smile widened, a spark of understanding and determination lighting up her eyes. "You're right. We're rewriting the rules, aren't we?"

"Now," Meryl grinned, a mischievous glint in her eye. "What are we?"

Mel laughed, the sound full and genuine for the first time that day. "MIILFs!"

Meryl looked at her, pride radiating from her like a warm glow. "Damn right, we are. Now, let's go make some magic happen."

As they rejoined the group, Laverne was in the middle of a heated debate with Natasha, their voices rising and falling like waves crashing against a gilded shore.

"Look," Laverne said, exasperation coloring her tone but her poise never faltering, "I'm not asking you to understand my journey. Lord knows it's been a wild ride with more twists than a Coney Island roller coaster. I'm asking you to respect it. And maybe, just maybe, learn a thing or two about running a successful business from someone who's had to overcome a few extra hurdles. Trust me, honey, in heels this high, every step is a triumph."

Natasha opened her mouth to retort, her eyes flashing with indignation, but Leah cut her off, stepping between them like a stylish referee.

"Oh, give it a rest, Nat," Leah said, her tone firm but not unkind. "The woman's got moxie, killer heels, and a business plan that could make Elon Musk sweat through his PayPal. In my book, that makes her MIILFF material. Besides," she added with a wink, "diversity is the spice of life. And let's face it, we could use a little extra spice around here."

"Here, here!" Krystal cheered, raising her teacup like it was a flute of champagne at a gala. The liquid sloshed dangerously close to the rim, threatening to spill over onto her designer blouse. "To new blood and old attitudes getting a much-needed makeover! L'chaim, bitches!"

As laughter filled the room, a symphony of genuine mirth and tentative acceptance, Mel caught Meryl's eye across the sea of perfectly coiffed heads. She mouthed a silent 'thank you,' feeling for the first time like she truly belonged in this eclectic, fabulous family.

Meryl winked back, a silent acknowledgment of Mel's place in this tapestry of strong, ambitious women. It was a small gesture, but it spoke volumes – of acceptance, of support, of the unbreakable bonds forged in the fires of shared dreams and struggles.

Laverne, sensing the shift in mood like a weathervane attuned to the winds of change, raised her perfectly manicured hand. The light caught on her rings, sending prisms dancing across the walls like a disco ball of success and sass.

"Now that we've settled that little kerfuffle," she announced, her voice carrying over the diminishing giggles, "who's up for a field trip to The Gilded Tassel? The first round of glitter shots is on me! And before you ask – yes, they're alcohol-free. A lady never loses her head, even when she's losing her clothes."

The room erupted in cheers.

CHAPTER NINETEEN
MORALLY BANKRUPT

Jericho, Jericho walls come down
Walls come down like Jericho
When I move it's an earthquake rumble
And I don't need to be humble
Mountain pose

The lyrics echoed in Leah's mind as she sat in her office, the weight of recent events pressing down on her like a designer straitjacket. The usual click-clack of designer heels echoed through CLUB MIILFF's marble halls, but today it carried an undercurrent of unease, like a discordant note in a symphony of success.

Suddenly, Mel burst into Leah's office, her face a storm cloud of worry, her Hermès scarf askew in a way that spoke volumes about her distress. "Leah, have you heard?" she gasped, breathless from what was clearly a sprint through the building. "Mimi's gone."

Leah's head snapped up from her laptop so fast she nearly gave herself whiplash. "Gone? What do you mean, gone?" Her voice was sharp, tinged with disbelief and a growing sense of dread.

"I mean poof," Mel said, gesticulating wildly, her bracelets jangling like alarm bells. "Vanished. Dropped off the face of the earth. Just like Maddie and Reese. And honestly, I am done." Her last words came out as a near-growl, frustration evident in every syllable.

Leah blinked, her perfectly manicured brows furrowing. "What do you mean, done?" She leaned forward, her elbows on the desk, giving Mel her full attention.

"Done," Mel repeated, pacing the office like a caged lioness. Her heels left little dents in the plush carpet, a physical manifestation of her agitation. "I am done with accepting blind direction. Something is going on. Mimi would have said something to me. We..." she paused, a flicker of vulnerability crossing her face. "We talked. A lot."

Leah's eyes widened at the implication in Mel's words. She'd always suspected there was more to Mel and Mimi's relationship, but now wasn't the time to pry. "Seriously," she muttered, running a hand through her perfectly coiffed hair, not caring if she messed up the $200 blowout. "This can't be a coincidence. Something is not OK."

Just then, Natasha sauntered in, trailing a cloud of cotton candy vape smoke that clashed horribly with the tension in the room. Her leopard print leggings and hot pink top were a jarring contrast to Leah and Mel's power suits. "What's with the funeral faces, ladies?" she drawled, taking a long drag from her vape. "Did someone cancel Botox Happy Hour?"

Mel rolled her eyes so hard it was a wonder they didn't get stuck. "Mimi is gone, Nat. Like, gone gone. Do you not understand the gravity of the situation?"

"Well, shit," Natasha said, plopping down on Leah's velvet chaise lounge with all the grace of a sack of designer potatoes. "That's more women disappearing than my ex-husband's hairline. And trust me, that was a rapid retreat."

Before anyone could respond to Natasha's ill-timed attempt at humor, the intercom crackled to life with Meryl's dulcet tones, smooth as silk but with an undercurrent of steel. "Ladies, emergency meeting in five. Bring your game faces and leave your questions at the door."

The three women exchanged glances, a silent conversation passing between them. Whatever was going on, it was big, and it was bad.

Five minutes later, the conference room buzzed with tension as the MIILFFs filed in. The air was thick with a mixture of expensive perfumes and nervous sweat. Meryl stood at the head of the table, resplendent in a power suit that screamed 'don't mess with me' louder than a New York taxi driver at rush hour. Ivanka lurked in the shadows like a Gucci-clad specter, tapping away on her ever-present iPad, her face illuminated by the blue glow of the screen.

"Now, I know there are rumors flying," Meryl began, her voice smooth as butter but with a hint of artificial sweetener. "And I am here to, of course, offer transparency."

Krystal, resplendent in a caftan that looked like it had mugged a rainbow, clicked her gum loudly. The sound echoed in the tense silence like a gunshot. "Doesn't feel transparent to me. Feels about as clear as my great-aunt Sadie's cataracts."

Meryl's smile tightened, looking more like a grimace. "Let's talk about alignment."

Natasha snorted, a plume of vape smoke escaping her nostrils like an irritated dragon. "Oh yippee, more corporate buzzwords! What's next, synergy? Paradigm shift? How about we circle back to the fact that our friends are vanishing faster than my will to live during this meeting?"

Meryl composed herself, though a vein throbbed visibly at her temple. "Yes, it's true." She paused, the silence stretching like an overworked facelift. "Mimi has decided to step down from her position. But let's focus on the positives, shall we? Her company is now fully integrated into the MIILFF brand, which means more opportunities for all of us."

Leah's eyes narrowed, her gaze sharp enough to cut diamonds. "And I suppose she just happened to sign over all her shares before disappearing into thin air? What, did she decide to join a convent? Take up extreme knitting in the Himalayas?"

Ivanka stepped forward, her smile sharp enough to cut glass. The clack of her heels on the marble floor sounded like a countdown. "Everything's perfectly legal, I assure you. Here are the documents if you'd like to peruse them." She dropped a stack of papers on the table with a thud that seemed to echo the finality of Mimi's departure. "We believe in full transparency, and you ladies are free to look at the data."

Krystal laughed, the sound as bright and artificial as her hair color. She made a trumpet sound as she fluffed her hair, a gesture so ridiculous it would have been funny if the situation weren't so serious. "Do I look like I read data? Honey, the only numbers I care about are my bank balance and my waist size, and not necessarily in that order."

As the meeting dissolved into murmurs and whispers, a sea of perfectly styled heads bowed together in conspiratorial huddles, Mel caught Leah's eye. A silent message passed between them, years of friendship allowing for wordless communication. Mel's fingers flew over her phone's screen, and moments later, Leah felt her own device vibrate.

My office. Ten minutes.

Leah texted back, her heart racing with a mixture of fear and anticipation. I'll be there.

Later, in the privacy of Mel's office, they huddled over Leah's laptop like two spies in a Cold War thriller. The glow of the screen illuminated their worried faces, casting dramatic shadows that seemed to underscore the gravity of the situation.

"Look at this," Leah whispered, pointing at the screen with a trembling finger. Her normally flawless manicure was chipped, a testament to her distress. "Every time one of our 'team members' disappears, there's a massive transfer of shares to a holding company. It's like watching a magic trick, except instead of a rabbit in a hat, it's our friends' livelihoods vanishing into thin air."

Mel squinted at the numbers, her designer glasses perched precariously on the end of her nose. "Holy shit," she breathed, the expletive sounding strange in her usually refined voice. "Leah, this is... This is huge. Meryl and Ivanka aren't just taking over; they're systematically pushing everyone out. It's like watching a corporate version of 'The Hunger Games,' and we're all tributes."

"It's like a corporate coup," Leah said, her voice trembling. She wrapped her arms around herself, suddenly feeling cold despite the warmth of the office. "But why? We were all successful already. It's not like any of us were hurting for cash or opportunities."

"Power," Mel spat, the word tasting bitter on her tongue. "Pure, unadulterated power. They're not satisfied with a piece of the pie; they want the whole damn bakery. Hell, they want to own the entire food industry."

A soft cough from the doorway made them both jump, Leah nearly knocking over her $500 ergonomic chair in surprise. Krystal stood there, her bedazzled glasses glinting in the low light like a disco ball at a funeral.

"I couldn't help but overhear," she said, her usual flamboyance subdued. She looked smaller somehow, without her usual larger-than-life persona. "And let me tell you, bubbles, this ain't my first rodeo with corporate sharks. I've swum with piranhas that had better dental plans than these two."

Leah's eyes widened, her jaw-dropping in a most unladylike manner. "Krystal, do you know something? Have you been holding out on us?"

"Let's just say I've been around the block enough times to know when something smells fishier than last week's gefilte fish," Krystal said, settling into a chair with a grace that belied her years. "I've been doing some digging of my own, and let me tell you, it ain't pretty. It's uglier than the bridesmaid dresses at my third wedding, and honey, that's saying something."

As Krystal laid out her findings, her bejeweled hands gesticulating wildly, Mel and Leah exchanged looks of growing horror. The pieces were falling into place, and the picture they formed was uglier than a Picasso painting in a funhouse mirror.

"I wonder which one of us is next," Krystal muttered, her voice uncharacteristically small. "I mean, let's be honest, it's probably me. I have not even read any of the contracts I have with the department stores. I have no idea what I even own. I just know I make money. Lots of it. But for all I know, I could be signing away my firstborn every time I autograph a shipment."

Mel's face paled, the color draining from her cheeks faster than a Spanx waistband snapping back into place. She started to think about her own contracts with Arthur. Ivanka had taken care of everything, her smooth assurances as intoxicating as the champagne they'd sipped to celebrate each deal.

"Oh my God, Leah," Mel gasped, her voice barely above a whisper. "Have you ever checked your book deal contracts?" She stopped, shaking her head in horror, her perfectly styled hair coming loose in her distress. "We've been so blind, so trusting. We're supposed to be smart, savvy businesswomen, and we've been played like a bunch of rookie Instagram influencers at their first sponsored post-meeting."

"We have to confront them," Mel said, her jaw set with determination. Her eyes blazed with a fire that could have melted steel. "We can't let them get away with this. We're MIILFFs, for crying out loud. We've faced down PTA mean girls and boardroom sexists. We can handle a couple of power-hungry Botox addicts."

Leah nodded her own resolve hardening. "But we need proof. Hard, irrefutable proof. The kind that would stand up in court and make even the most jaded New York judge sit up and take notice."

"Leave that to me, darlings," Krystal said, a mischievous glint in her eye that hadn't been seen since her disco-dancing days. "I may be old, but I've still got a few tricks up my sequined sleeve. You don't survive three divorces and a stint on a reality TV show without learning how to dig up dirt. By the time I'm done, we'll have enough evidence to bury Meryl and Ivanka so deep, they'll need a submarine to see daylight."

The next day, armed with a file full of damning evidence thick enough to stop a bullet, Mel and Leah marched into Meryl's office like two avenging angels in Louboutins. The MIILFF matriarch looked up from her desk, her smile faltering at the determination in their eyes. For a moment, she looked old and tired, like a wax figure left out in the sun too long.

"Meryl," Leah said, her voice steady despite her racing heart. She could hear the blood pounding in her ears, but her words came out clear and strong. "We know what you and Ivanka have been up to."

Mel slammed the file on the desk with enough force to make Meryl's designer paperweights jump. "Lying to us! Cooking the books, strong-arming our sisters out of their companies, building your own little empire on the backs of our hard work. Did you really think we wouldn't figure it out? We're not just pretty faces, you know. Some of us actually read the fine print."

Meryl's facade cracked, fear flashing in her eyes like lightning in a storm. For a moment, she looked like a cornered animal, dangerous and desperate. "Ladies, please. You don't understand…"

"Oh, I think we understand perfectly," Leah cut in, her voice as cold as a December morning in Central Park. "The question is, do you understand that we're about to blow this whole operation sky-high? By the time we're done, the only empire you'll be running is the snack bar at the federal penitentiary."

For a moment, silence reigned, heavy and oppressive as a Versace comfort blanket. Then, to their shock, Meryl crumpled, her shoulders sagging under an invisible weight. It was like watching a designer soufflé collapse in real time.

"Please," she whispered, her voice barely audible, a far cry from the commanding tone they were used to. "Please, just... give me a chance to explain. It's not... It's not what you think."

Mel and Leah exchanged glances, thrown off balance by this sudden vulnerability. It was like seeing your teacher cry or catching your parents in a moment of weakness. Unsettling, to say the least.

"You've got five minutes," Mel said, crossing her arms. Her stance was defensive, but there was a flicker of something else in her eyes. Curiosity? Concern? "Make them count. And make them good, because right now, the only thing stopping us from going nuclear is the fact that orange is definitely not your color."

As Meryl opened her mouth to speak, the air thick with tension you could cut with a Ginsu knife, they all knew that whatever came next would change CLUB MIILFF forever. The walls of their gilded empire were crumbling, and in the rubble, they might just find the truth they'd been seeking all along.

CHAPTER TWENTY
CORPORATE SPILL

My heart is paralyzed
My head was oversized
I'll take the high road like I should …
How could you leave on Yom Kippur? Plank. Hold, breathe

The tension in Meryl's office was thick enough to cut with a Prada stiletto. Mel and Leah stood, arms crossed, as Meryl sank into her plush leather chair, looking smaller and more vulnerable than they'd ever seen her.

"Well?" Leah prompted, her voice sharp. "We're waiting for this grand explanation of yours."

Meryl's perfectly manicured hands trembled as she reached for a crystal decanter. "I think we're going to need something stronger than coffee for this conversation."

As she poured three generous glasses of amber liquid, Mel's eyebrows shot up. "It's barely noon, Meryl."

"Trust me," Meryl said, her voice hollow, "you're going to want this."

She downed her drink in one gulp, then looked up at them, her eyes shimmering with unshed tears. "What I'm about to tell you... it goes beyond CLUB MIILFF. It goes to the very heart of who I am."

Leah and Mel exchanged glances, then perched on the edge of their seats.

"I wasn't always... this," Meryl gestured vaguely at her impeccable outfit and the opulent office. "Before all this, I was just a secretary. Barry Arthur's secretary, to be precise."

"Arthur?" Mel interjected. "As in, your ex-husband Arthur?"

Meryl nodded, a bitter smile twisting her lips. "The very same. But he wasn't my husband then. He was my boss. My very powerful, very manipulative boss."

Leah's eyes widened as realization dawned. "Oh, Meryl, you didn't..."

"I didn't," Meryl confirmed, pouring herself another drink. "At first."

She closed her eyes, lost in memories. "He tried a bunch of times. I always turned him down. But he was persistent, always hovering, always finding excuses to keep me late at the office."

Meryl took a shaky breath, her gaze distant. "And then, my very abusive boyfriend beat me so badly I finally had the courage to break up with him. I came to work with bruises I couldn't hide, and Arthur... he was kind. For the first time, he seemed to see me as a person, not just an object."

She paused, taking another sip. "A month later, I realized I was pregnant. With Ivanka."

The silence that followed was deafening. Mel was the first to break it. "But everyone thinks Arthur is Ivanka's father."

"That's because Arthur decided it would be so," Meryl explained. She closed her eyes, lost in the memory.

Young Meryl stood in Arthur's opulent office, her hands shaking as she clutched a piece of paper. Arthur looked up from his desk, his eyes narrowing.

"Well? What is it? I have a meeting in ten minutes."

Meryl took a deep breath. "Mr. Dunway... Arthur... I'm pregnant."

Arthur's face went through a range of emotions - shock, anger, then a calculating look that made Meryl's blood run cold.

"Is it mine?" he asked, his voice dangerously low.

Meryl shook her head. "No, it's... it's my ex-boyfriend's. The one who..."

"The one who beat you," Arthur finished. He stood up, circling his desk like a predator. "Well, this is quite the predicament you've found yourself in, isn't it, Meryl?"

"I... I don't know what to do," Meryl admitted, her voice barely above a whisper.

Arthur's laugh was cold. "Oh, I think you do. You're here because you want something from me. Money for an abortion, perhaps? Or a raise to support your little bastard?"

Meryl flinched at his cruel words. "No, I... I just thought you should know. I'll be resigning, of course."

"Resigning?" Arthur raised an eyebrow. "And go where? Do what? You're a knocked-up secretary with no skills and no prospects. Who do you think would hire you? Who would want you?"

Tears welled up in Meryl's eyes. "I... I'll figure something out."

Arthur's voice softened, becoming silky, persuasive. "Or... you could stay. I could take care of you, Meryl. Of your child. I could give you both a life you've never dreamed of."

Meryl looked up, hope and suspicion warring in her eyes. "What... what do you mean?"

"Marry me," Arthur said simply. "Let the world believe this child is mine. I'll give it my name, my fortune. And you... you'll want for nothing."

"But... why?" Meryl asked, bewildered.

Arthur's smile didn't reach his eyes. "Let's just say it serves my purposes. But make no mistake, Meryl. Without me, you're nothing. A cheap whore who got herself knocked up. No one would have you. I'm offering you the world. Are you smart enough to take it?"

Meryl's voice was hollow as she finished recounting the memory. "And I took it. God help me, I took it."

Leah leaned forward, her brow furrowed. "But why? Why would he do that?"

Meryl laughed, a hollow sound devoid of humor. "Oh, he had his reasons. At first, it was appearances, mostly. I was young, and pretty, and he could mold us just how he wanted. And then, I found out that Arthur is sterile. His previous wife left him when she found out she would never conceive, and to protect his image, he married me immediately and claimed my unborn child as his own. Can you imagine the scandal if it got out?"

"Does Ivanka know?" Mel asked softly.

Meryl shook her head, fresh tears spilling down her cheeks. "No. And that's... that's the crux of it all. I've spent my entire life trying to protect her from the truth. Trying to give her the life I never had. And in doing so, I've become... this."

She gestured at the damning file on her desk. "Everything I've done, every underhanded deal, every manipulation... it's all been to secure Ivanka's future. To make sure she never wants for anything."

Leah's voice was gentle when she spoke. "But Meryl, at what cost? You've hurt people. Good people."

"I know," Meryl whispered. "God, I know. But... I owe Arthur everything. Without him, Ivanka and I would have been nothing. Nobody. And Ivanka... she idolizes him. She does whatever her parents tell her to do. If she knew the truth..."

Mel reached out, placing a comforting hand on Meryl's arm. "Don't you think she deserves to know?"

Meryl looked up, her eyes filled with fear. "And have her hate me? Think of me as some... some loser young knocked-up mom who trapped a rich man? No. I can't. I won't."

Just then, a gasp from the doorway made them all turn.

Ivanka stood there, her face pale as a sheet, her iPad clutched to her chest like a shield. She was frozen, shock overtaking her features as the weight of what she'd overheard settled in.

"Mom?" Her voice was small and childlike, a stark contrast to her usual confident demeanor. "Is... is it true? What you just said?"

Meryl's face drained of color, her carefully constructed world crumbling around her. "Ivanka, sweetie, I can explain…"

But Ivanka was already backing away, shaking her head in disbelief. "No. No, this can't be... Dad's not... I'm not..."

Before anyone could stop her, she turned and fled, her heels echoing down the hallway like a retreating army.

Meryl slumped in her chair, looking utterly defeated. "Well," she said, her voice barely above a whisper, "I guess I deserve this, don't I."

Leah and Mel exchanged looks of shock and sympathy. The web of lies had finally unraveled, but the truth it revealed was more complex and heart-wrenching than they could have imagined.

As the weight of the revelation settled over the room, they all knew that nothing would ever be the same again. The future of CLUB MIILFF hung in the balance, and the path forward was anything but clear.

Meryl looked up at Leah and Mel, her eyes red-rimmed but determined. "I have to go after her. I have to make this right."

As Meryl stood, straightening her designer suit-like armor, Leah and Mel nodded in silent support. They watched as Meryl, the formidable leader of CLUB MIILFF, walked out of her office not as a powerful businesswoman, but as a mother desperate to reconnect with her daughter.

The truth was out, and now they all had to face the consequences of years of secrets and lies. But perhaps, in the rubble of their carefully constructed facade, they might find something real and lasting – a chance for genuine connection and healing.

CHAPTER TWENTY-ONE
MIILFFS IN MOTION

Hashem Moloch

Hashem Melech

Hashem Yimloch Leolam Vaed

The ancient Hebrew words echoed through the MIILFF headquarters, a reminder of the strength and resilience that had brought them to this moment. The conference room, once a battleground of corporate intrigue, now pulsed with an electric energy of sisterhood and determination. It was as if the very walls were breathing, alive with the collective power of women ready to reclaim their destiny.

Leah stood at the head of the table, her eyes blazing with a fire that could melt steel. Her perfectly coiffed hair seemed to crackle with energy, each strand a conduit for the passion in her heart. As she shared the events that had unfolded, including Arthur's nefarious plans, her voice rang out clear and strong, like a clarion call to arms.

"Ladies," she began but was quickly interrupted by a loud, theatrical cough from Laverne.

Leah paused, a smile tugging at her lips. She looked at Laverne with respect and admiration, acknowledging the diversity that made their group so powerful. With a nod, she rephrased, "MIILFFs, we have been played and messed with, "she announced, her voice ringing as clear as a crystal champagne flute. "But it's time we turned the tables. It's time we show the world what happens when you underestimate the power of a mother – or any woman – interested in launching financial freedom. We may not have our financial freedom, but we have something better. We have a group of powerful professionals that can help us all be free."

The room erupted in cheers, a cacophony of designer heels stomping and manicured hands clapping. It was a war cry of the fabulously fierce.

Natasha leaned forward, her vape forgotten for once. A sharp glint in her eye replaced the usual cloud of fruity smoke. "What's the plan, boss lady? I've got enough fire in me to torch Arthur's whole empire, metaphorically speaking, of course."

Mel jumped in, her voice trembling with excitement. "We've got to reach out to everyone. Maddie, Mimi, all of them. We're stronger together. Like a designer handbag collection – each piece is beautiful on its own, but together? Unstoppable."

"On it," Krystal chirped, her bedazzled phone already in hand. The rhinestones caught the light, sending tiny rainbows dancing across the room. "I've got more contacts than a drag queen has wigs. By the time I'm done, we'll have a network bigger than Arthur's ego."

Laverne raised an elegantly manicured hand, her eyes twinkling with mischief. "Did someone say wigs? Don't forget, girls. I've got connections in places Arthur wouldn't dare step foot in. We can use that. The Gilded Tassel isn't just about tassels if you know what I mean." She winked, sending a ripple of knowing laughter through the room.

Leah nodded appreciatively, feeling a surge of gratitude for the diverse talents of her MIILFF sisters. "Perfect. Laverne, work your magic. We need all hands on deck. Your connections could be the ace up our designer sleeves."

Just then, the doors burst open with a dramatic flair that would make Broadway jealous. Ivanka strode in, her eyes red but her jaw set with determination. Gone was the daddy's girl, replaced by a woman ready to forge her own path. "I want in," she declared, her voice ringing with newfound strength. "I've been Daddy's little girl for too long. It's time I became a real MIILFF."

A cheer went up around the room, so loud it seemed to shake the chandeliers. Meryl, standing in the corner, looked at her daughter with a mix of pride and apprehension. The years of secrets and lies she was melted away, replaced by a tentative hope.

"Honey, are you sure?" she asked softly, her voice carrying the weight of years of protection and sacrifice.

Ivanka strode over and took her mother's hands, her touch gentle but firm. "Mom, you sacrificed everything for me. Now, it's my turn to step up. We're going to take Arthur down, and we're going to do it legally. It's time I used everything he taught me against him."

Natasha whooped, punching the air with enthusiasm. "Hell yeah! Law and order, MIILFF style! We'll make those courtroom dramas look like kindergarten squabbles!"

As the room erupted in laughter, a sound of pure joy and liberation, Mel's phone buzzed. Her eyes widened as she read the message, a smile spreading across her face like sunshine after a storm. "Ladies, you won't believe this. Maddie and Mimi are in. All the way." She beamed, relief and excitement radiating from her. "They're rallying the troops as we speak."

At the mention of Mimi's name, Mel's heart did a little flip. The thought of seeing her again, of finally having the chance to explore the connection they'd always danced around, sent a thrill through her body.

Leah clapped her hands, the sound cutting through the excited chatter like a starting gun. "Alright, MIILFFs, listen up. Ivanka, what's the deal with those weekly NDAs? Time to spill the tea, and I'm not talking about our organic chai lattes."

Ivanka's face darkened, a storm cloud passing over her features. "They weren't NDAs at all. They were profit share agreements. Every week, you've been signing over a piece of your company. It was like a corporate vampire, sucking away your lifeblood one signature at a time."

A collective gasp filled the room, followed by a wave of angry mutters. The betrayal stung, but it only fueled their determination.

"But," Ivanka continued, a sly smile spreading across her face like butter on hot toast, "I think I know how to nullify them. Dad may have taught me every trick in the book, but he never thought I'd use them against him." Her face grew serious, the weight of the task ahead settling on her shoulders. "I need to pull an all-nighter to see if this can work before D- Arthur pulls another fast one over us. It's going to be me, a gallon of coffee, and enough legal documents to wallpaper the Empire State Building."

Krystal cackled, the sound like a fabulous witch casting a spell of empowerment. "Oh, honey, that's what happens when you underestimate a woman. Especially a MIILFF! We're like fine wine – we only get better with age, and we pair well with cheese and revenge."

Laverne raised her champagne flute, the bubbles racing to the top like their rising spirits. "To take back what's ours! May our stilettos be sharp and our minds even sharper!"

As the women clinked glasses, the sound ringing out like a battle cry, Leah turned to Meryl. The vulnerability in the older woman's eyes was a stark contrast to her usual iron-clad demeanor. "You ready to come clean about everything? It's the only way to break Arthur's hold for good. It's time to step into the light, Meryl. We've got your back."

Meryl took a deep breath, looking around at the supportive faces surrounding her. Each woman had her own story and struggles, and they were all united in this moment of truth. "I... yes. Yes, I am. It's time to break the chains of the past and step into a future of our own making."

The next few hours were a whirlwind of activity, a hurricane of girl power and determination. Phones rang off the hook, legal documents flew back and forth, and the air crackled with feminine energy so potent it could power a small city.

Leah rushed to her office, her mind already spinning with plans. "Get me every single influencer in the tri-state area," she commanded, her voice ringing with authority. "It's time to make our story go viral!" Within hours, she had every influencer from Instagram models to TikTok stars ready to share the "tea" about Arthur's attempted coup.

Mimi, her heart racing at the thought of reuniting with Mel, gathered her team to call local event halls. Her voice, usually reserved for planning perfect weddings, now spread groundbreaking news about how Arthur tried to undermine a powerful group of Club MIILFFs. "We're not just planning a party, ladies," she declared, her eyes sparkling with determination. "We're planning a revolution!"

Mel, her writer's mind in overdrive, created mini scripts that read like a Hollywood blockbuster. "Leah, share these scripts with your media company," she said, handing over a stack of papers that seemed to glow with potential. "Let's give the storytelling power to the MIILFFs. We're not just changing the narrative; we're rewriting the whole damn book!"

Maddie, finally free to reclaim her nursing empire, coordinated with healthcare professionals across the city. Her voice, warm and compassionate, rallied support from doctors, nurses, and medical staff. "We're not just fighting for our businesses," she reminded them. "We're fighting for the right to care for our community on our own terms."

As the sun began to set, casting a golden glow over the city that seemed to herald their impending victory, Ivanka burst into the room. Her hair was disheveled, dark circles under her eyes, but she was waving a stack of papers like a victory flag. "We did it!" she cried, her voice hoarse but triumphant. "The agreements are null and void. You all own 100% of your businesses again! Arthur's house of cards is tumbling down!"

The room erupted in cheers and hugs, a tidal wave of joy and relief washing over them all. Natasha broke out a fresh round of champagne while Krystal started an impromptu conga line that snaked around the conference table.

Amidst the celebration, Meryl cleared her throat. The room fell silent, all eyes turning to the woman who had been both their leader and, unknowingly, their adversary. "There's one more thing," she said, her voice quiet but firm. "I need to come clean about Ivanka's parentage. It's time the truth came out. No more secrets, no more lies. Just the raw, unvarnished truth."

A hush fell over the room as Meryl told her story. It was a tale of abuse, chaos, and trauma but also of hope, love, and the birth of a young girl born into possibility. As she spoke of her struggles, her sacrifices, and her unwavering love for her daughter, the room listened in rapt attention. It was the story of a mother doing whatever it took to give her child the life she never had. When she finished, there wasn't a dry eye in the house.

Ivanka, tears streaming down her face, wrapped her mother in a fierce hug. "Mom, I don't care about any of that. You're my hero. You hear me? My hero. You faced the world alone and came out fighting. That's the MIILFF spirit!"

Mel raised her glass, her voice thick with emotion. "To Meryl, the original MIILFF. Taking on the world to give her daughter a better life. You showed us what it truly means to be a mother interested in launching financial freedom."

"To Meryl!" the room echoed, the sound swelling like a wave of love and acceptance.

As the celebration continued into the night, a symphony of laughter, clinking glasses, and the sweet sound of victory, Leah found a quiet moment with Mel. They stood by the window, looking out over the glittering city that now seemed full of endless possibilities.

"Can you believe it?" Leah mused, her voice soft with wonder. "We really did it. We're free. We took on the big bad wolf and came out on top."

Mel grinned, bumping Leah's shoulder playfully. "Free, fabulous, and ready to take on the world. Watch out, universe. The MIILFFs are coming for you! We're not just leaning in; we're kicking down doors and taking names!"

Laverne sashayed over, draping her arms around them both. Her touch was warm and accepting a physical reminder of the bond they all shared. "And don't you forget, we've got a grand opening to plan. 'The Gilded Tassel' waits for no woman! It's going to be the hottest spot in town, a testament to what happens when women support women."

As laughter and plans for the future filled the air, Mimi approached Mel, her eyes shining with unspoken emotions. "Hey, stranger," she said softly. "I hear you've been busy saving the world."

Mel turned, her heart skipping a beat at the sight of Mimi. "Just another day in the life of a MIILFF," she quipped, but her voice was tender. "I missed you, you know."

Mimi smiled, taking Mel's hand. "I missed you too. More than you know. What do you say we make up for lost time?"

As Mel and Mimi moved to a quiet corner, their heads bent close in intimate conversation, Leah looked around the room. Maddie was excitedly discussing plans for her newly reclaimed nursing business. Krystal was regaling a group with tales of her undercover work, her bedazzled glasses flashing in the light. Natasha and Laverne were deep in discussion about a potential collaboration between their businesses.

And in the center of it all stood Meryl and Ivanka, their arms around each other, years of secrets and lies washed away by the tide of truth and love.

One thing was clear: CLUB MIILFF was back, better than ever, and ready to show the world what happens when you mess with a mother interested in launching financial freedom. They had faced their demons, confronted their past, and emerged stronger for it.

The night sky twinkled with possibilities, each star a reminder of the dreams they dared to chase. For the MIILFFs, the future had never looked brighter. They had rewritten their story, turning a tale of corporate greed into an epic of sisterhood, empowerment, and the unbreakable bonds of friendship.

As the celebration continued, the energy in the room was electric with possibility, they all knew that this was just the beginning. The world had better watch out – the MIILFFs were coming, and they were ready to change the game, one fabulously fierce step at a time.

Epilogue

Andrew slouched in his Italian leather armchair, his fingers dancing across the remote control with the nervous energy of a man consumed by bitterness. The 85-inch flatscreen that dominated his bachelor pad flicked through channels at a dizzying pace, each image barely registering before being discarded.

Suddenly, he froze. There she was again. Leah. Her megawatt smile beamed out from the screen, her perfectly coiffed hair gleamed under the studio lights as she confidently delivered another episode of her wildly successful show, "The Corporate Minute."

"Another episode of Leah and her stupid corporate minute," Andrew muttered, his voice dripping with disdain. He took a swig of his craft beer, grimacing as if the taste of his own jealousy was souring the artisanal hops.

Leah's old colleague had been watching her meteoric rise to the top with a toxic mixture of envy and resentment. It burned him to see her success, each of her achievements feeling like a personal slight against him. The memory of their shared past at the company gnawed at him like a persistent toothache.

At one point, she had even reported to him. Andrew's lips curled into a sneer as he recalled their last interaction, Leah's words echoing in his mind with painful clarity: "I will never do business with someone who doesn't align with my core values."

The audacity of it! The sheer, unadulterated gall! Who did she think she was, turning down his "mentorship"? Didn't she know he was doing her a favor by deciding to guide her career?

Leah had seen right through his narcissism, her keen intuition cutting through his facade like a hot knife through butter. She wasn't afraid to speak her mind, even if it would cost her career. Andrew remembered how she often stated she had given up much more than money to live authentically.

Andrew hated that. He hated her integrity, her courage, and her refusal to play according to the old boys' club rules. But most of all, he hated how she had succeeded despite – no, because of – her principles.

"I am sick of seeing her face everywhere," he growled, hurling the remote at the TV. It clattered to the floor, batteries spilling out like the last dregs of his professional reputation.

Suddenly, it hit him. An idea so devious, so deliciously under-handed, that it made his lips curl into a smile that would have made a cartoon villain proud.

With renewed energy, Andrew sprang from his chair and rushed to his state-of-the-art home office. He began furiously typing on his Z-Scaler, his fingers flying across the keyboard with manic intensity. Twenty minutes later, a cynical grin crept up his face, transforming his features into a mask of smug satisfaction.

The screen popped up to a brand-new website he had just purchased. The logo, garish in its attempt at femininity, proclaimed: W.I.F.I – "Women In Financial Independence."

Beneath it, in a slightly smaller font: "We are inclusive of all who identify as women."

And there, at the bottom of the page, was the coup de grâce: "Founded by CEO: Andrew." With a flourish, he crossed out the 'W' from "Andrew" and replaced it with an 'A'.

"My name is Andrea now," he announced to his empty apartment, his voice pitched higher in a crude approximation of femininity. "And I identify as a WIFI, pronounced 'wifey', but just a woman in financial independence." He smirked, pleased with his own cleverness.

Andrew – no, Andrea – leaned back in his ergonomic chair, basking in the glow of his deviousness. In his mind, he was already seeing the headlines, the confusion, the controversy. He could practically taste the chaos he was about to unleash.

"Ok, Club MIILFF," he purred, his voice dripping with malice. "You may have had your moment, but Leah, you and W.I.F.I are about to go to war."

With an exaggerated flourish, he tossed his non-existent long hair over his shoulder. The imaginary hair flip, in his mind, was the perfect punctuation to his declaration of war.

As he sat there, bathed in the blue light of his computer screen, Andrew felt a surge of twisted excitement. This was his chance to reclaim the spotlight, to stick it to Leah and all those "empowered women" who had left him in the dust. He didn't care about the ethics of it all – in his mind, all was fair in love, war, and corporate takeovers.

Little did he know, his actions were about to set in motion a chain of events that would shake the foundations of the financial world and test the bonds of the MIILFF sisterhood like never before.

The battle lines were drawn. Club MIILFF versus W.I.F.I.

Authenticity versus deception. Leah's hard-earned wisdom versus Andrew's bitter scheming.

As the first light of dawn began to creep through his window, Andrew was still there, hunched over his keyboard, crafting his persona of "Andrea" with meticulous care. He was building a house of cards, each fabrication adding to the precarious structure of his plan.

But in his arrogance, in his burning desire for revenge, Andrew had overlooked one crucial fact: he was about to go up against a group of women who had already faced down corporate sharks, overcome personal demons, and emerged stronger for it.

The MIILFFs had fought for their happy ending once before. And if Andrew thought they wouldn't fight just as hard to protect it, he was in for a rude awakening.

As the sun rose over the city, casting long shadows across Andrew's cluttered apartment, the stage was set for a showdown that would redefine the meaning of women's empowerment in the corporate world.

The war between Club MIILFF and W.I.F.I was about to begin. And only one side could emerge victorious.